500 HOSTELS IN THE USA
(& CANADA & MEXICO):

Backpackers
&
Flashpackers

Hardie Karges

Copyright © 2013 Hardie Karges

All rights reserved

ISBN: 0988490595

ISBN 13: 9780988490598

Library of Congress Control Number: 2013905606

Hypertravel Books,
Los Angeles, California

Table of Contents

Table of Contents

Table of Contents

Table of Contents

Preface:
Elephant in the Room and the
#Paradigm Sh**t

Every project has its revelations and its epiphanies, and this one is no exception. What started out as a simple project of journalistic drudgery to pay some dues, hopefully pay some bills, and build my platform and brand™ as a traveler and writer, has ended up as something much more, facilitating a "movement" which I find to be a very positive development in the history of travel, maybe even the history of the world. Then when simple introductions to simple directories became theoretical abstracts of some very brick-and-mortar histories and geographies, the skeleton took on flesh and the mission took on meaning. The mission overtook the math, and the work became a joy.

As I begin the second phase of this project—USA, Canada, and Mexico—after having completed the two European editions, it's certainly appropriate to see where we've been and where we're going. Much of the travel basics, of course, are the same, so continuing readers: please bear with me. Many readers will buy this one book only and need the info. As before, it's brief—just the essentials. I won't insult your intelligence by offering to help you choose a backpack. By now the directory listings have pretty much become a format, and the geographical/historical abstracts—a point of pride for me in this series—have become fairly concrete.

The hostel concept is largely associated with Europe—especially Western Europe—and is generally well-known, so its emergence in Eastern Europe should come as no surprise. But now we're moving into a different region, which, certainly in the case of the USA and Canada, is very similar to European culture. But what about Mexico, which is quite different and historically much poorer? How does the hostel concept translate to that region? America, after all, is slow to get on the bandwagon, so there's no guarantee... And we're talking about 'real' hostels, now, remember, not just cheap rooms. Well, I have good news and bad.

America is the elephant in the room, of course, the biggest economy in the world, and by far the biggest consumer of goods and services. Well, I'm happy to report that the USA is finally — finally — starting to get hip to hostels, though it's still got a long way to go. It's mostly still in the old Boy Scout/YMCA-era of 'youth hostels' in which a few establishments — mostly HI affiliates, thank you — are scattered about the landscape in areas that aren't, and never were, appropriate for hiking and camping, the usual American/Boy Scout-style preference. The few 'flash-packer' modern hip 'new era' hostels that exist are mostly limited to large cities, mostly on the two coasts, particularly ones that Europeans and other internationals are likely to visit — New York, Miami, Los Angeles, San Diego, San Francisco, Portland, and Seattle. Here hostels are making rapid gains and are starting to approach typical European numbers, double-digits or close to those numbers of hostels per city... and I don't list Motel 6's.

Canada is similar to the USA, differing in only a couple of ways. For one thing, they have a far greater penetration into the actual wilderness, especially in the Rockies, offering some unparalleled opportunities there. For another thing, some of their urban hostels are not exactly up to modern standards. "Flashpacker" implies a qualitative upgrade of facilities, too, you know, not just a backpacker's increased income and age or the urban — as opposed to rural — orientation with opportunities for partying. Toronto in particular has some hostels that I just can't include here because of their uncertain quality. Selecting only hostels with websites usually weeds out the dubious operations, but not always, not here. I don't want to list a hostel 'unvetted.' Montreal is better, not surprisingly considering its general orientation *tres European*. Still there are some gaping absences as in the US, particularly in that vast open middle region, so not all that much different from the US.

So what about Mexico, then, you ask? First, let me ask you a question. Without looking at the table of contents, guess which city in these three countries has the most hostels. New York, maybe? Vancouver? LA? How about Mexico City? Yes, there are over twenty of them here, and most of those are less than two years old, so they're definitely starting to 'get it.' Heading south from there the plot only thickens, on a proportionate basis, and the Mexican Caribbean coast if counted as one market would surely rival Greece. And for better or worse, most of those are party hostels, so they're definitely 'getting it.' The surprising thing is that the quality is so good, maybe a few in the 'funky old Mexico' mode, but most quite acceptable to European modern standards (and some of the best websites I've seen in my life, *hmmm*)... And there is heavy penetration even in the north-central region, so Mexico is definitely ahead of both the USA *and* Canada in the modern 'flashpacker' trend in hostels. You heard it here first: Mexico is very hostel-friendly. And whatever comprehensiveness this compilation lacks — not much — it might be in the count for Mexico. I've scrounged pretty hard to document the USA and Canada.

After all the hostels and cities and countries are counted and documented, though, the question still remains of not only what constitutes a good hostel, but what constitutes a "real" one. This is no trivial matter and as author of this book and facilitator of this mission, I feel it is up to me to answer this. I really have no choice, since otherwise the book goes off on tangents everywhere, and ultimately goes nowhere. A hostel is more than a cheap hotel, or we wouldn't be having this discussion. So I decided at the outset that a hostel would simply be defined as a place of lodging that offers shared rooms, i.e. dorms. That should keep the upscale pretenders and transient riff-raff out. Still that doesn't quite do it, not really, not totally. Some places that offer shared rooms still aren't real hostels and some places that don't... really are. So it's more than that, but not easily quantifiable.

There's something of an *esprit de corps* — a group spirit — that inhabits a real hostel, along with its many and various travelers, something that derives from the long meandering trail, and is not limited to the destination. That's something that used to be *de rigueur* to backpack-style travel back in the early days, long before hostels became important outside their West European homeland, and one of the most attractive parts of the expedition, really. That was a different era, of course, but it's that feeling that's important, that feeling and that authenticity and that honesty, that acceptance and union of self with the universe, however alone, however together. That's what defines us, and that's what unites us. Thus backpackers and hostels inherit a little bit of last century's '60's ethos of peace, love, and understanding, simply by the act of showing up... on the other side of the world.

But the last thing I expected in the process of compiling these simple compendia was to create a prototype of a new type of travel guide, so that's a happy accident. For me at least, this book has redefined the concept of what a travel guide should be: lean and mean and polished to a light sheen. This is the kind of guide I'd use, one that provides the most important info, without planning the actual trip for you; one that provides crucial information, without so much presumption and subjectivity as to who you are and what you'd want to do. I personally don't need to know hypothetical routes; I know how to use a map. And I don't need to know bus schedules; those change. And I certainly don't need to know where to eat (unless it's famous); you're insulting me. I don't want someone else's trip; I want my own. When a guide tells me where to eat, I'll make a point of eating somewhere else. Mostly I just need to know options of where to sleep.

Above and beyond that, what I need most is some inspiration to know which places are worth visiting in the first place. I hope that this book will facilitate that. One of the happy offshoots of this project, indeed, is that now there is a quantitative standard to decide how "cool" a place is — and therefore worth visiting, maybe even hanging for a while. Just count the number of hostels (proportionate to the overall population, if you want to be fair and derive a true mathematical coefficient). As it has been up until now, you could read a 500-page guidebook, and still not necessarily have a good feel as to which places were "hip," *genial, sympa,* anything but a boring, hurly-burly generic city, cold but not cool (despite their 'local experts'… but no locals). Now you do, because hostels are nothing if not cool. Why else would people like me stay there when we have choices? Just become I'm a backpacker doesn't mean I'm broke. I'm flash-packing, baby. The new gap year comes at age fifty-five. Now you know; C U there.

Introduction

What is a hostel? Originally they were places, mostly in Europe, where students could sleep for cheap on extended country outings, frequently established at appropriate intervals over and about the landscape and which corresponded more or less to the amount of distance a student might hike or bike in the course of a day. Since those outings usually occurred in the summer when schools were otherwise uncommitted, the schools themselves became the logical place for seasonal conversion. That still happens sometimes, but not much. The concept has expanded dramatically over the last decade, for a variety of reasons, no doubt; among them: rising hotel prices, rising restaurant prices, and — drum roll here, please — Internet. For the rise of Internet has not only made advance booking widely accessible for both hostel and traveler, but it also became a reasonably-priced accommodation where a traveler would almost certainly have access to that same Internet. This fueled an explosion which is still happening to this day, and has barely scratched the surface yet in many places.

In the introduction to my book "Hypertravel: 100 Countries in 2 Years," I wrote, "Not surprisingly, hostels are least prevalent in places where cheap hotels and guest houses are most available, such as Southeast Asia." I just might have to return the Cuban cigar I received for that brilliant observation. At last count Singapore had over forty hostels, and even very-reasonably-priced Bangkok almost as many. In contrast Boston, in the good ol' US of A, has... what, two or three? I guess hostels, with their shared rooms, just aren't American. But all that's changing, especially in New York, with some of the highest hotel rates in the world. Even in Africa, especially southern Africa, the concept is huge and growing, and in Latin America, they're fairly abundant. The only problem is that there exists something of a flexible and locally-influenced definition of what really makes a good hostel, so that this guide to North American hostels will reflect those considerations.

What any good hostel should have, by my own current standards, are: 1) cheap dorm beds, 2) English language, 3) a kitchen, 4) storage lockers, and 5) easy access to Internet. Of course within each of those categories there exists significant margin for deviation, but a place of lodging should make the effort to at least offer something in each of these five basic requirements in my humble opinion. Other things you can expect that probably wouldn't be considered "amenities" include DIY bedding (you know how to make a bed, right?) and the likely absence of a towel (though many have it, but charge). For purposes of this guide I had to decide what ultimately defines a hostel, and for me that's the shared rooms. It's nice, for me at least, if they have private rooms also, but if they don't have dorms, then they won't be in this book. This book is not intended to be totally comprehensive, either, so don't be surprised if you don't see your favorite party hostel in Toronto. This book tries to be selective, a little bit, at least. There's a reason for that, several of them, in fact.

There are some downsides with hostels in general, though usually no more than the sometimes institutional nature of them or uncertain housekeeping. A bigger problem can be location, especially where they're rare. That hostel may be located far from the center and not obvious even when standing right in front of it, no sign of the business conducted within, many of them no doubt informal in their business approach. There are other issues, also, such as the once-standard curfews which are rapidly disappearing. Then there are the also-once-standard age limits, also in decline, though still there sometimes, the main problem being one of where to draw the line. I've seen upper limits anywhere between thirty-five and fifty-five. That's problematic for those of us who hold non-discrimination dearly *and who are already over fifty-five*.

Other hostels are more creative and limit ages only within dorm rooms. That sounds reasonable, especially given the other discrimination issue: most dorms are of mixed sexes, though female-only dorms are not uncommon. It's mostly cool and without problems, but still these are valid issues to consider. Most backpackers' hostels simply have no age limit, and that's the way it should be, I feel. Any problems can be dealt with on an individual basis. Another related problem is that in some cities of Alaska (for example) hostel beds rank as decent long-term accommodations for some individuals and even families, who attempt to live there. Most hostels rightfully attempt to discourage this, as they should. Hostels are not transient hotels, after all. I try to weed those places out. It gets worse sometimes.

Introduction

Some small hostels are barely staffed, if at all, absentee landlords showing up to let you in and set you up, then disappearing until the next guest shows up. Some legitimate "boutique" hotels do that, too, where they rightfully value their own private lives, but others are merely renting a flat and calling it a hostel, with little regard to your needs or that of their neighbors. If you book in advance, and they demand to know your arrival time, then that's a good clue. If they call you in advance, that's another. If they have no website (the ones here do) and the hostel-booking site has few pictures, then that's another. Unfortunately a place with a bad rep can simply change its name and start all over as if nothing ever happened. I try to weed those places out of this guide and include only "real" hostels.

With this guide you can contact hostels directly before committing any money, which is good. That way you can do some weeding, too, even at the last minute. You can't do that with most hostel-booking sites, which for some hostels is their only connection to potential customers. *I don't recommend booking on a hostel-booking site less than three days from your estimated time of arrival.* There's a good chance they won't have your reservation yet. That's why this book exists. Contact the hostel directly, by e-mail probably okay if two days out, by phone if less.

For better or worse, consolidation is setting in to the hostel scene rapidly, and the days of the "hippie hostel" may be numbered. The most obvious manifestation of this trend is the appearance of hostel chains, not only within a city or country, but in multiple cities across a region. I think that this in general is good, as it establishes standards of services and expectations. The downside, that quirky little mom-and-pop operations may get squeezed out, is probably misplaced, since many of those places wouldn't rate very highly on my hostel-meter anyway, and the current "Air BnB" trend is probably more suitable to their offerings. Many of those would not even be found in this book, since they don't have websites. Conversely, some of the biggest chains may not be represented for every one of their branches here. I try to strike a balance between standards and individuality. Just because a place calls itself a hostel is not enough for me.

A word should be mentioned about HI, Hostelling International, which is often affiliated with YHA and such. This is the original hostel chain, and largely responsible for the existence of hostels, or at least their smooth transition from those early schoolboy barracks into modern backpackers' party hostels. They are a membership organization and you will need to pay an extra charge to stay there if youre not a member. When you've done this a half-dozen times or so, you'll be a member. But this guide is not about HI, though some are listed, particularly the ones that offer beds on the major hostel-booking sites. In fact they could probably fill a book larger than this of only their member hostels worldwide, though many of their branches are open only seasonally, and subject to their own qulifications and definitions, so I won't concentrate much on them. For better or worse, they tend to represent the old school of "youth hostels" more than the modern era of "backpackers."

By the way in some quarters (e.g. the cover of this book J), a hostel itself is known as a "backpackers," short for "backpackers' hostel," I assume. Make a note. Also, pricing gets elaborate and confusing, and frequently changing, so are included here for comparison purposes only. Just know that in the US and Canada a dorm bed will likely run $20-50 and Mexico usually less, maybe as little as half that. And for a private room, you'll have to pay that same price for two to three people, regardless of how many actually occupy the room. You should be aware that in some places — Mexico comes to mind — you might do better price-wise for a small cramped private room in one of the chock-a-block centers of budget accommodation around the bus station. That's when some of the other considerations come in, like Wi-Fi or a kitchen or…

The best thing about a hostel I've hardly even mentioned yet, because it's a hard thing to quantify, and that's the people you'll meet. Even an old geezer like me needs some social intercourse (yep) from time to time, and given our frequent differences from the locals, travelers are the next best thing. In out-of-the-way places like Tonga or Tanzania, that's priceless. In places like Calgary, that's "Party Time!" Don't forget to wear protection (for your ears, that is). So that's pretty much what hostels aka "backpackers" are all about. But what's a "flashpacker," you ask? I think that's what you become when you've been a backpacker too long and can't stop, maybe a little older, hopefully a little wiser, more up-scale and maybe less group-oriented, i.e. hard-core, or maybe 'die-hard.' I guess that's me. Some flashpackers may also be more urban and less interested in remote locations than in partying in the pubs. That's not me. By extension, and given the close connections between the words and concepts of 'backpacker' and 'flashpacker,' an upscale hostel can be referred to as a 'flashpackers,' too.

If you're American, then you're probably wondering why this historic trend seems to have skipped over the good ol' USA. Actually it didn't, really. Ever heard of the YMCA? They're always booked up in New York. This book's for you. America's indeed the last to get in on the modern trend, but I expect that to change very soon. I think many Americans just can't see themselves staying in dorms, but that's half the fun if you're young, and a surefire way to meet people. So what makes this book better than a website for booking hostels? That's like comparing apples and oranges. For one thing, we give you the hostel's own website and/or e-mail address and phone number for direct communication. So, not only can we be more objective than a booking site that receives a commission, but a booking site may show a hostel to be full when a call or e-mail to the hostel itself will get you a bed immediately. For another, we try to include only the "real" hostels, hopefully without bad reviews. But if they don't have dorms, then they won't be here, and likely the same result if they have no website.

This is intended as an introduction and complement to the vast online resources and hopefully a broader view. Still, hostel-booking sites are invaluable for feedback, specific information and special promotions, and I urge everyone to consult them. Two of the bigger ones that I know best are *www.hostelbookers.com* and *www.hostelworld.com*, though there are many others, and *www.hostelz.com* acts as something of a "kayak" for them all, so that's good. Then there's the membership-only *www.hihostels.com*, but as mentioned before, that's more likely an old-school "youth hostel," so not really the focus here, though some are included. If you're looking for something out in the countryside, they may even be best. But we're getting ahead of ourselves. This is a travel guide (both time and space), as well as a hostel guide. If you're a novice traveler, then you need to know some basics first.

Travel Basics & Traveling Around North America

Transportation: Buses, Trains, & Planes

There's nothing more basic to travel than the actual transportation. In general that means buses, trains, and planes, right? Well, for international travel, especially inter-continental travel, that mostly means planes. But which planes? Well, you can just go to a travel agent and they'll be happy to do everything for you, but if you're a do-it-yourselfer like me, then you probably want a little bit more control over the process than that, and you probably wouldn't mind knowing how it works, so that you can tweak it to your own tastes and proclivities. The good news is that with online booking you can do that. I do things in the booking process I wouldn't dare ask an agent to do. The first thing to decide is where and when you want to go, and then start pricing.

First determine what's the nearest major hub city (usually the largest and the lowest price) in the region you're going to, or coming from, and then compare to that. Major hubs around the world include London, Paris, Cairo, Istanbul, Dubai, Johannesburg, Delhi, Bangkok, Singapore, Lima, and others. In the US: New York, LA, San Francisco, Chicago, Miami, Houston, Dallas and Atlanta are the biggies, in no certain order. If you're traveling abroad and want a multi-city route, then carefully check for airlines that hub in one of the cities on your route, for instance for LA-Paris-Cairo-LA, you'll definitely want to check Egyptair and Air France, in addition to a multi-line site or two. Expedia and the like can and will book any multi-segment flight on multiple airlines, very convenient!

Are you still with me? So what's next? In the old days I'd check the Sunday travel section in LA, New York, or San Fran papers—the library'd have them if the newsstands didn't—and start looking for deals from "bucket shops," i.e. consolidators. They'd buy large blocks of seats to re-sell and always undercut the airlines themselves, who were limited by IATA rules and regs in what they could do. Then I'd get on the 800# line and start chatting with someone with a thick accent in Times Square or Union Square or Chinatown or on Broadway downtown somewhere, trying to get the right price. It'd never be the price in the ad, of course, but I'd try to get close. Then I'd make payment and ticketing arrangements to be mailed back and forth, money order for them, paper ticket usually Fedexed to me, very "old school." Or if I were stopping in that same city on my way out of the country, then I might even stop in their office, if I could squeeze into the cramped spaces they typically occupied. Those ads have mostly disappeared.

It's easier than that now. Some of those places still exist—Flight Center and STA Travel come to mind as multi-city biggies—but rarely will they have better deals now than what you could find for yourself on the Net. I usually go to one of the major multi-airline travel sites like Expedia,

Introduction

Travelocity, etc. (or Kayak will pull them all up for you to compare) and see who flies where and when for how much. Then I'll go to the website of one or more of those airlines and compare prices. They're not always the same, and as often as not the multi-airline site will be cheaper, BUT... that might change tomorrow. The airline's own site will change less, but the multi-line sites can somehow magically splice together several airlines for multi-city itineraries, all at very reasonable prices. They also have hotels, too, but if you're reading this book, then that's probably not your thing. One advantage to Expedia, etc. is that prices include tax; with airlines' own sites, you'll probably have to continue to checkout to know the final price. Don't be fooled by false low numbers.

When to buy? You know that already, don't you? The sooner you buy, the better the price, right? Not necessarily. Of course you need to check as far in advance as possible just to budget yourself, but I'd say start checking prices seriously no later than three months before your anticipated travel date. But don't buy yet. Online sales are usually immediate, so you probably want to keep options open as long as you can. A travel agent might make a reservation for you and let you pay later, so that's one advantage to working with them. Then if you find it cheaper yourself, you can cancel with the agent or simply let it expire. Don't book the same flight as the one your agent's already booked, though. That gets messy.

I'd still advise you to do some legwork, regardless. If your dates are flexible, then check prices for each day a week before and after your preferred date; they'll probably vary, but Tuesday and Wednesday will usually be cheapest. Check again a week later; it goes fast when you get the hang of it. If prices start going up for Fridays then you might want to go ahead and purchase that Wednesday flight. If not, then wait. I've seen some major discounts right at two months out, if the seats aren't selling quickly enough, so wait until then if you can, fifty-nine days out if your plans are firm enough. If not then start monitoring every day or two. A large group can sell a flight out quickly. Once a seat is gone, they rarely come back. It's not like the old days when reservations were made, then frequently cancelled.

If you're trying to book a frequent-flyer flight from an airline, generally a tiered system will charge you a certain amount of miles for Europe (50K+/-), Asia (75K+/-), Africa (100K+/-), etc. without any advantage necessarily to the major hubs. Those hubs may have stiffer fees and taxes, too, and the award usually doesn't cover that. I'm searching flights to Africa from the US right now, hubbing out of Europe. It costs 40,000 frequent-flyer miles to fly to either London or Lisbon. London's fees are $600; Lisbon's are $200. Go figure. If you're using frequent-flyer miles attached to a major non-airline bank card, then usually now those convert to 1% of the cost of the flight, i.e. 50,000 miles = $500 flight, booking through their agent. Poke around the site first, though, and you might find a minor partner that still uses the old tier system (like Bank of America's Canadian partner). You'll likely get more that way if you're flexible with dates. Whew!

It might be worth a line or two about "free flights," the subject of more than one budget travel book, and a fairly simple deal. Deal is, usually, that you apply for an airline-based credit card, which will typically give you 30-50,000 free miles as incentive; all you have to do is spend probably $3-5000 within the first 3-5 months. Of course you have to have good credt, too. So it's a pretty good deal if you fit those circumstances, but of course, you can only do that a limited amount of times, and beware, the first year may be free of annual fees, but the second usually is not, and they can easily run up to $100 — or close to it. As long as you cancel the card before the fee is actually due, then you're probably okay, though, so check your bills carefully. That's enough on that subject.

North America is likely the easiest place in the world for travel: the routes are well traveled and the carriers are well-known. Unfortunately that means there aren't many cheapo airlines like Europe these days. I think we went through that phase already. Mexico does, though, and in Mexico it takes some extra planning regardless. For buses in the USA and Canada, it's pretty much Greyhound, though if there happens to be a Megabus route in your area, then that could be cheaper. They came and went in some area with little notice or fanfare, complaining of low ridership, when no one had ever really heard of them. It's hard to ride a bus that you don't know exists.

There are lots of Mexican buses and shuttles in the US, but Anglo-Americans don't ride them; they don't know about them. Greyhound service through Canada is pretty well universal, though I don't think there's service to Alaska. There are shuttles up around the Arctic Circle from Fairbanks to Dawson City via Chicken and Tok, but you should reserve in advance. Google. It should be beautiful. I wanted to do it in 2006, but just didn't have the time.

For you hostel-hoppers in Southern California, there's good news, too, a service that will now not only connect you between the major centers of Los Angeles and San Diego, but to intermediate points and your final destination: *www.thehostelhopper.org*, a good deal.

There are multiple bus lines in Mexico, and they're all good. You can reserve and buy e-tickets in advance with some of them if you want, but I probably wouldn't recommend it, unless it's a major holiday. Otherwise seats are plentiful, and buses are frequent, and some may be more convenient than others, the higher-priced e-ticket buses using their own terminals away from all the others. I've also had some paid reservations go unconfirmed, so not worth the hassle in my opinion. Trains in Mexico have been largely discontinued over the years, except for some specialized routes like Copper Canyon, which is too bad, since they were pretty nice, and cheap, too.

I'm happy to report that Mexico is getting on the cheap flight bandwagon, though, more than the US or Canada, though you'll probably need to google for your specific city needs. International flights into Mexico are likely cheaper on American carriers, if they exist for your particular destination. They all go there, Canada, too. Air Canada is okay, especially if you have Bank of America frequent-flyer points and partner on Aeroplan. Alaska Air is one of the better carriers on the West Coast and into Mexico.

Visas: Consulates, Passports, & Letters of Introduction

Depending on your nationality and where you're going, you might need a visa, which is a stamp in your passport that is your permit to enter a specific country. They have to be applied for at an embassy or a consulate. Do that two to three months before travel, also, if possible. You already knew you needed a passport, right? Don't worry; it can usually all be done by mail, but allow plenty of time, and make sure your passport has at least six months of validity from the date you plan to enter the last country on your itinerary or they might not let you in, or require a 'special fee.' Visas can sometimes be picked up on the road, but get as many as you can in advance from your home, especially if you live in a major city that has embassies and consulates.

Nothing is certain out there. There are companies that will do it for you, but it can get quite expensive. Google hard, but the best source for knowing what visas you'll need (if you're American) is probably *http://travel.state.gov*. Other countries have their own. If you're doing the work yourself, then check the websites of the countries whose visa you need to get instructions.

This part's easy for North Americans in North America. If you're an American or Canadian traveler, then the continent is your oyster, no visas required. And if you're European, then it shouldn't be much harder, just make sure you do that online security thing before you get on the plane. East Europeans will have to check for their particular country. Mexicans, you know the drill better than I; sorry about that. Of course, if you Americans or Canadians plan to go further south into Guatemala or beyond, then you might want a visa, if you plan to stay very long and cross several borders, save you the cost of a $10 one-off entry card at each border, and one visa should cover four countries, all the way down to Costa Rica. All Americans need passports even for Canada and Mexico, now, too, don't forget; nothing else will do.

Money: Currencies, Exchange Rates, and ATM's

Money is important when traveling, of course, the more the better, but you don't have to actually carry it all with you. In general I recommend ATM's, since traveler's checks are almost extinct, and you usually have to go into a bank to cash them, as opposed to the generally more available exchange booths. The problem with ATM's is that they aren't everywhere in the world, believe it or not, and service charges can be high. If you plan to travel a lot, it's worth getting a bank account that doesn't charge much for foreign transactions. You need cash, too, of course, and a credit card for emergencies, so I recommend a mix of them all, a few traveler's checks, too, if you can get them. You don't want to get stuck with extra foreign currency, though Euros or Pounds (or Canadian dollars) are not so bad since easily changeable almost everywhere. There's an art to using up your worthless currency. Buy gifts at the end of a trip to use up extra currency. The last few days change just what you need until you cross the next border. Small denomination dollars (or whatever your currency) are good for those border areas.

Change money at established locations unless you're desperate, and count your money carefully whether at an exchange house, at a bank, or on the street. But first look at the posted rates, both of them. There's a "buying" rate and a "selling" rate. Unless you're leaving the country and want dollars or Euros or whatever back, then the buying rate is the one you're getting, the lower of the two. If it's a good rate, then there should be no more than 2-3% difference between the two. If it's more than five I'd probably pass, unless I'm desperate. Also check to see if there are commissions or extra charges. In the US or Canada there usually are. Use ATM's. Use any leftover currency immediately at the border or first stop of the new country you're entering, or you might be stuck with it. Some currencies are largely non-convertible, e.g. PNG *kina*. Use 'em up. Never exchange money at a US airport on the way out. It's a rip-off, same in West Europe. If I need to carry cash in US Dollars, then I usually prefer fifty-dollar-bills, since they'll get as good of a rate as hundreds, are usually prettier, and are easier to cash in a pinch. Old worn bills won't pass.

Strangely enough given our significant similarities, I've more often had problems getting Canadian currency than almost any other. Many ATM machines there simply won't take US cards, bummer. I guess familiarity breeds contempt. On the other hand, your credit card is not likely to have any problem there, so you might want to have it handy. No, they don't want USD and forex is a rip-off. There's no problem in Mexico. *Cambios* are plentiful.

Communications: Cell-phones, Cards & Computers

I think this is where the phrase, "it's complicated," originates. If you're European or from most anywhere else in the world besides the US, then it's easier. But America is slow to get on the worldwide GSM digital network standard for cell phones, and that's what you need, that and a multi-band phone, one that can handle both 1900 (Am) and 1800 (rest of world) band frequencies (Korea and Japan also have their own if that's your home or destination). Most new phones will make the switch automatically; if not, then look in the menu for something like settings>network>band, and then choose the one you need. If you're already with AT&T, T-Mobile or another GSM network in the US, then your phone should work all around the world, albeit with high international roaming charges. You may need to activate 'world service' first. Poke around the website, though, and you might find some special arrangements for particular countries. Barring that, if you're going to be in any one country for very long, then it's worth buying a local SIM card and putting it in your phone.

What's a SIM card? Simply put: that little thumbnail-size circuit-board accessible through the back of the phone is your number and all the information that goes with it, including your calling history. It's easy to switch, but you'll probably have to "unlock" your phone first if it's American. American cell-phone services are traditionally monopolized, with prices to match. If that's what it takes to produce iPhones, then so be it. If you're switching services in the US (after fulfilling your contract), then request the company to unlock it. If you're tech-savvy, you might even find tools online to unlock it yourself. Otherwise, go to the sleazy part of town in some sleazy city (say, Toronto) where people do things they're not supposed to do and look for signs around cell-phone shops that say "phones unlocked," or something like that. Buy a local SIM card for ten or fifteen bucks, stick it in, and then start blabbing. Some might even be worth keeping, if they give you a better international rate than your US phone would.

Smart phones are too new for me to have the skinny worldwide. Buy the next edition, and I'll promise to be up-to-date by then. This is a real breakthrough, obviously, to have a local map in your hands constantly and ready to use. It's not that easy, though, not yet anyway. For one thing, there are the high roaming fees mentioned earlier. For another, the G3 system doesn't exist everywhere in the world yet, much less G4, so simply buying a new SIM card and sticking it in is not necessarily a quick easy solution. Stay tuned. As a lover of maps, I find this development exciting if only for that reason. After all, who do I want to call in most countries that I travel in? But maps are something else entirely. Of course using a phone with G3 internet to tether to your laptop is tantalizing, but not free. In many hostels WiFi is free. That was my original inspiration for them.

Actually phone calling cards are still popular and useful, but you don't always need actual cards. Sometimes all you need are the PIN number and the access numbers, so you can do that online with much greater choice than in Chinatown. Ones that allow you to call all over the world from the US are dirt cheap. Cards that allow calling from anywhere to everywhere might be harder to find and more expensive. Read the fine print carefully. Of course even then you'll need a local phone to call the access number, so maybe not worth the hassle for a traveler.

The best option generally these days is to use Skype on your Internet device: anywhere everywhere cheap no hassle, all you need is WiFi for calling out or even receiving calls whenever you happen to be online. For someone to call you anywhere any time, though, you still need your own number. Skype rates may finally be climbing now, but there are copycats with similar services to compare to. As for Internet in general, Wi-Fi is an international standard, so available everywhere, of course, but don't expect them to be everywhere for free. Since you're reading this book, though, your odds are decent with the places listed here. One nice thing about G-4 cell-phone-style Internet is that it'll be everywhere there's phone service and quality should be comparable to WiFi. Then those GSM (GPRS) modems that connect to the USB port of your Internet device should truly be competitive with ADSL high-speed Internet. As with cell-phones if you're going to be around a while, it might be worth it to buy a local SIM for your GSM modem.

There is one new development regarding cellphones worth mentioning and that is the availability of "world phones," specifically intended for world travel, an option worth considering, especially for Americans, maybe even Europeans and others, particularly for those who need several different numbers for several different places. As mentioned before, most Americans don't have GSM phones, which is the world digital standard, and roaming's not cheap with ATT and T-Mobile, even if you do. Now you can buy a UK SIM card and/or phone and travel the world with a +44 number, and not only pay for the service in US dollars, but pay no monthly fees at all.

If you pay after each use, then the rate is no bargain, but if you pay in advance, then it's not so bad, comparable to top-up service in developed countries, some with the option to receive calls in many of the world's countries absolutely free, and especially good for West Europe if you're American, and vice-versa. It gets better. Many of these services offer the option of having two or more numbers available for use on the same SIM card, with some considerations as to which number is better for which countries, though generally it would be the "global" number for an American—usually a UK number, though I've also seen Belgian and Estonian ones.

Some services — particularly the Estonian — will even allow you to choose many numbers for use around the world, charges often only accruing if you need a permanent number. I've had a post-paid number for years for emergency world use, but now I have a pre-paid one, and so far it looks good. I may even use it for service in the US full-time. For someone who doesn't talk much, it's very economical to only pay for what I actually use, with no monthly fees, or only a dollar every two months to buy the number, and use the phone at least once or twice a year to keep the SIM card active. Some phones not only allow two numbers on one SIM card, but also accept two SIM cards simultaneously! How's that for service? Unfortunately most of them aren't smart-phones, boo hoo. Here's a website for more info: http://www.prepaidgsm.net/.

The US and Canada are on the same phone system, of course, so that ensures good quality, but doesn't mean that calls will be free or even cheap. Still it should be cheaper than most other countries. Ditto for Mexico, not same phone system but should be cheap, though not necessarily. Country code there is +52. Canada and Mexico are both on the American 1900 frequency band, so theoretically you wouldn't even need a quad-band phone as long as you have world service with your AT&T, T-Mobile, or other GSM service. Ask about world service if you don't know. In a Mexican border-town, though, you might not want it, as your phone will want to lock on to the strongest signal, even though the Mexican will cost you more than the American one. Alaska and Hawaii should be normal American service. For WiFi, neither Canada nor Mexico will feature it as ubiquitously as the US, but that's one reason we stay in hostels, right? Generally 800/866/877/etc phone numbers cannot be used internationally, except with Skype.

Security: Rip-offs, Scams and Insurance

Of course you need to be careful at all times when traveling. You're especially vulnerable when walking around with a full pack. Don't waste time in that situation; don't do it after dark; and don't even think about it in Port Moresby, PNG or even in New York City, for that matter. And spread that money around, on your body, that is. Don't keep everything in one easy place. Losing a little is much better than losing a lot. Got a passport bag? Don't dangle it off your neck, either inside or out. Put your arm through it and conceal it snugly under your armpit, ready to be locked down tightly, with your arm. Carry that daypack in front or off your side; a thief in a group following you closely behind can riddle through your bag without you even knowing it. Be careful with strangers; maintain some distance. If anyone gets too close, or follows behind for too long, then stop! Let him pass.

Put that wallet in your front pocket; butts aren't so sensitive usually. Avoid crowds in general; but if you're in a crowd and feel a bump, then grab your bag or wallet immediately. You might feel someone else's hand there. That's how pickpockets work. Don't confront them; they're fast. You won't even be sure who it was. Tight passages are the same. Pickpockets wait there to pass through at the same time as you. Deal is: when you feel the bump, you won't feel the grab. If you're walking around after dark, consider carrying something gnarly in your hand, like an umbrella or a flashlight or a nasty-looking set of keys. A belt with heavy buckle that slides right out of the loops fast works well. Most thieves want to work quickly, but not all. There are slow scams and false fawning fraudulent friends, too. Remember to wear protection.

This is all for deterrence, remember; you never want to ever actually get into a tangle. If someone acts menacingly toward you and they're not yet close, then run like Hell. If they pull a gun or knife, then give them whatever they want. Your life is worth more than your iPad. In the unfortunate event that you do get robbed or mugged, don't panic. Go to the police, get a report, and start the work of canceling credit cards and getting a new passport. That means going to the nearest consulate or embassy and telling them you need an emergency temporary passport. They can usually do it in a few hours. If they imply otherwise, then talk to someone else. It can be done; I've done it. Hopefully you've got a copy of the passport; that helps. A birth certificate also helps. Remember to allow extra time at the airport of your departure, as they'll need to fix the entry stamp that's now in your lost passport. Hopefully you've got a few bucks stashed away. That helps. Don't be shy about asking for help. Get religion; that helps.

Political security is another consideration, and for an American the most thorough update is from the site already mentioned: *http://travel.state.gov*, then divide by half and that's about right (they're more cautious than your mama). Keeping up with the news is a good idea, especially for the countries where you're going. Last decade's war zones can be great travel bargains, though, like Belfast, Belgrade, Beirut, and... give Baghdad some more time. Simply put: be careful and don't take chances. An ounce of prevention is worth a kilo of cure. I'm not a big insurance guy, considering it in general to be a rip-off, but others have differing opinions. If you're booking a flight on a multi-line booking site, it'll be available there, sometimes on individual airlines' websites also. Some promote it heavily to pad the bill; you might have to opt out to get it off the bill. If you're going somewhere dangerous, that ups the ante a bit, of course.

Mexico is undergoing a wave of violence unparalleled in its history, so you could certainly be excused for having some concerns, BUT... the good news is that you're not likely to run into any of that. For one thing, that mostly pertains to very specific areas, most of them in the far north, especially on the border. You always need to be aware of your surroundings, of course, and try not to draw attention to yourself. You'll draw enough attention regardless. And you're just as likely to be a victim of violence in any large city of the US... or Canada. I'm serious. You're at greater risk disembarking at the Greyhound bus station in LA at midnight than any city in Mexico that I know of. If you're traveling by bus in the US, you probably should time your trip to arrive during daylight hours. Not every station has taxis waiting, or bus service. That information is all available online in advance.

Health: Vaccinations, Food and Drugs

You know the drill, right? Multiple rounds of shots wherever you go and for the tropics, don't forget the prophylaxis, right? To be honest, I've never gotten most of those shots, just the ones required by law, but it would be irresponsible of me to suggest that you do the same. Tropical areas are certainly the problem, so require extra caution, though yellow fever is usually the only shot actually required by law. If you have to get that in the US just to get a visa, then it'll set you back a cool $100-150. If you can get it on the road somewhere, then it might be as little as ten bucks. Ask at public health centers; sometimes they'll jab you right at the border, just to facilitate matters. Some vaccines seem not much better than the disease, so use your judgment. Malaria prophylaxis is easy enough if you're actually entering a malarial area, but so are mosquito nets. Don't ever have sex with locals without a condom.

If the food seems strange at first wherever you happen to be, then go slow with it, allow your bacteria some time to adapt. You should experiment, though, since some of the local delicacies are delicious. Just make sure that foods have been recently made and are best served hot. The nose knows. Ask locally about water quality, though it's usually easy enough to drink bottled water or boil tap water first to be sure.

As for recreational drugs, I've got a simple rule: nothing never no way no how—just kidding! But you should be aware of the risks. A lot of countries take simple possession of marijuana as a *very serious offense*, punishable by death, or you might wish you're dead by the end of it. I would not advise traveling with ganja anywhere in the world. That smell is hard to get out. If you just gotta' have a little smoke once in a while, then I advise you to befriend the hipsters wherever you end up, which carries its own set of risks. Better yet, why not just quit for a while? You might be amazed how much easier you catch that buzz when you get home. It's the contrast that counts. Being stoned all the time is no fun. Of course more and more countries are legalizing it, so that's good. Latin America may soon be a dope-friendly continent, what with Uruguay already legal and others considering it, most of them tolerant, Europe too. Asia is intolerant.

Unfortunately more and more Muslim countries are outlawing alcohol, so it's the same thing. Take a break; you'll enjoy it more if/when you start back. Many Muslim-lite countries are growing more fundamentalist. Your best bet there are hotels, which are often considered international zones exempt from local standards. Remember that wherever you are, especially poor countries, that as a rich (yes) foreigner, you're vulnerable, so be careful. If you've just got to get a buzz once in a while, you might consider checking out the pharmacies. Things are legal overseas that are controlled tightly in the US; be creative, and read instructions carefully. It might be a good time to fix that cough. The cough syrup overseas is excellent. Check the ingredients. It even cures coughs... sometimes.

If you've got a serious drug habit, then you really should de-tox. It doesn't go well with travel. You should be careful even when drinking with locals. Mickeys do get slipped, and so do roofies. Finish that drink before going to the head. Don't accept drinks already opened, in bars or buses or trains, whether alcohol, milk or water. It's better to offend than to get robbed. Let me be clear that I do not advocate any drug use myself (I rarely if ever even drink now) but I understand the desire, so wish to see it done responsibly. But if you think you'll stay in hostels because those sound like cool places to smoke pot, then think again. I've never—I repeat, **never**—seen so much as a joint smoked at a hostel. Alcohol, yes, that's fairly common in hostels, but not pot.

Health concerns in the US and Canada are minimal, of course, and Mexico should pose no real problem in the cities and northern areas. If you're going to be spending time in the Lacandon jungles of Chiapas, then you might want to get the full round of shots and prophylactics. Malaria is no fun. Neither is hepatitis, so avoid tap water and that means ice, too, especially in those outdoor drink stalls in Tampico with the temperature topping 95F/35C and you figure you've been such a good boy for the last month so what the hell, go ahead and have one. Don't do it. I'm sure health and sanitation has improved in Mexico over the last thirty-five years. Casual marijuana use is no bigger deal in Canada than the US, and not much different for Mexico.

Cultural Considerations: Sex, Religion and Politics

Among Western or westernized countries it's no big deal, of course. Our informality is our calling card and our stock in trade. That's not true elsewhere, though it's tricky to intuit. Some of the rockingest whoringest countries can be quite conservative amongst locals, Thailand for instance. In Thailand you'll rarely see locals kissing in public, though in the international zone, you'll see much more than that, of course. Vietnam has no such taboo, and couples hang all over each other in parks. Act conservatively until you know the local mores. As corny as it sounds, we are ambassadors to the world, and I'd like to think we have a larger mission to bring people together through our highest common denominators.

Think hard before taking on a local girlfriend, a good girl, that is. It'll take some time and patience. Women won't have such a problem, but just be warned that many local guys will only want a quick fling with a wild Western woman. If and when it comes time to do the nasty, always keep a few millimeters between you and the object of your affection. Anything else would be the ultimate in foolishness. Politics is always a bit dicey to discuss in public unless you know your host and his or her inclinations. Some places there can even be legal repercussions, such as Communist countries and a few Muslim ones. Tone it down. Most cultural considerations usually boil down to something much more mundane, though. Shoes are customarily removed when entering houses, and sometimes buildings, in much of the world, whether Buddhist, Hindu, or Muslim, so please comply willingly. They take it seriously.

Canada is culturally almost identical to the US, so you know the love game as well as I. Let me know if you ever figure it out. Mexico is a "whole 'nother country," of course, so moderate your expectations. If you're a guy hoping to party with some Mexican cuties, you'll likely be disappointed... unless you like prostitutes. If you're a woman who likes Mexican guys, then you'll probably find yourself to be quite popular. Go slow with fast friends. Guys up to no good are not like the ones in no hurry. They usually like to cut to the chase. Prostitutes traditionally operate in "*la zona*," but that's changing, and girls might operate in any disco or bar, but I've never seen anything like TJ's red-light district elsewhere, not that I've been looking...

What to Pack: Clothes, Communications and Cosmetics

There's one simple rule: travel light. I personally carry a day-pack and a laptop computer bag only, no matter the destination, no matter the length of the trip. Forget the monopoly board; forget the five-pound toilet kit; and most of all: forget the library (including all those 500-page travel guides), except for this book, of course. A laptop or Nook or Kindle can hold all the books you'll ever need *or you can buy whatever you need whenever you need it*. That is true of almost everything. A few changes of clothing are all you need, and a change of shoes, preferably a variety of things that can be layered as needed. The trick is to wash clothes as you go along, every chance you get, very easy if you have a private room with sink, not so easy in a dorm, but they frequently have machines there, so do everything up whenever you get the chance, except the set you're wearing.

Wear those hiking boots when you actually travel, so you never have to pack them. Add a pair of flipflops or kung fu slippers or sneakers to that, and you're set. My secret item is a down padded vest, which will compress to almost nothing, and keep you very warm in the coldest situations (plus cushion your pack and be a bus pillow and…). Add a long-sleeve shirt, and a T-shirt or two, which can go under or alone, a couple flowery shirts to accompany those pheromones you'll be sending to the opposite sex, a pair of long pants, a pair of shorts and a pair for swimming, and you're set. Use small 100ml bottles for toiletries (per carry-on restrictions), a needle and thread, a small umbrella, a power adaptor for multiple countries (and dorm rooms with few sockets), a luggage lock, and… That's about it. Don't forget the Internet device. I know you won't.

If you're touring the entire North American continent in one trip, then you'll need to prepare for many different climates, of course, depending on the season and the altitude. Mexico has the highest peaks between Denali (Mt. McKinley) and South America. The hurricane season that blasts the southeast US coast affects Mexico, too, especially the Yucatan and Caribbean which is in the direct path of the more southern trajectories. If you're going to Alaska or the Yukon in the summer, then I envy you. If you're going in the winter, then God bless you. Mexico is pretty warm year-round from the Tropic of Cancer (that curved line that runs through Mazatlan) on down.

Travel Guides: Books, Maps and Internet

Guidebooks and Internet should work together for travel, but I think the relative importance is reversed. Instead of carrying a huge book around for your basic travel information and then using Internet to book hostels and play around on FaceBook, I suggest using Internet for basic travel information, too. Not only is the amount of information enormous, but it's updated constantly. This book can help finding hostels, too, whether you have Internet or not. For me large travel guides are not only an anachronism, but were never really necessary in the first place, maybe to read up on beforehand, but not to travel with. I've rarely traveled with one. Most travel is largely intuitive, and a book removes you from that. I would recommend it only in the most remote or linguistically-challenging places, when it might really aid survival.

One thing I DO like to travel with are maps. But they're cumbersome, hard to find and harder to handle. Once again Internet is perfect for this, every place in the world available from multiple views. I look at maps the way some people look at pornography; I can't get enough of them. One of the main problems with hostels, of course, is that they're hard to find, so that you almost need detailed destructions at some point regardless. I'm hoping that this guide can help bring hostels into the mainstream and promote some standardization. There will always be local and regional quirks as to how they operate. This is a book to carry with you.

How Hostels Work

But for a few small differences, a hostel works the same as any hotel, guesthouse, lodge, B&B, whatever. I won't insult your intelligence by explaining to you that basically you're paying for a place to sleep. Where it differs mostly from the others is that at a hostel you'll likely be sharing your room with a bunch of others in similar bunk beds. That creates a unique set of circumstances which requires some attention to detail. First there's the booking process. If you're staying in a dorm, then often you'll have to decide how many roommates you want. The more roommates you have, the less the price generally.

Hostels are generally booked in advance; otherwise they can be hard to find. That's once reason this book exists, to help with last-minute walk-ups and walk-ins. That's very possible where hostels are properly signed and conveniently located. Call first if it's a long walk or ride. I never made an advance room reservation in twenty-five years. It's nice to be spontaneous. This way you can look at it first, too, never a bad idea if you've got the time. Don't do that around midnight. Advance booking might still be cheaper, and hostel-booking sites may be cheaper than the hostel's own website. Shop and compare. If you book in advance you'll probably need to pay a deposit in advance by credit or debit card, usually 10%. Upon arrival, you'll need to pay the rest. I'll try to tell you here which take plastic, but don't count on it. Carry enough cash, just in case. If you want extra days, advise in advance if possible. For a long stay, you might want to book two or three places two or three days at the time if you don't know them well. That way, if you get a bad one, then you'll be out soon.

Obviously there is an inherent security situation with hostels that needs addressing and some malcontents seem to have figured out the basic equation faster than those in charge. I mean... I hate to be a spoilsport, here, but just because somebody stays in a hostel doesn't mean he's honest and loyal. I don't know about you, but that's my life there in that backpack, and I'm hesitant to just toss it there on the floor and walk out assuming it's secure. That's why every hostel needs lockers, and you need a lock. Lockers don't always have them, and if there are no lockers, then try to lock your pack directly to the metal frame of the bed or something similar. No thief wants to jimmy a lock if he doesn't have to; he'll take what's easiest. If you're in the room with others, don't show a lot of valuables; the walls have eyes.

Curfews are largely a thing of the past, except in the original "youth hostels," but beware the mid-day lockout, which some places impose "for cleaning," though you and I both know they're just saving on employee costs, maybe the entire profit margin at a small place. There's a good side to that, of course: the place is secure while you're out. Conversely, since the demise of the curfew, hostels have become popular places to party, sometimes facilitated by the hostel management themselves (beware in Calgary, or Tallinn, or London, or...). If the kitchen is full of liquor bottles, then that's a good sign. If there are hordes of Homies, i.e. local non-travelers, hanging out, then that's another. The yobs coming in to London from Hounslow for the weekend tend to look and act differently than the travelers from the Continent. Another sure sign is when a hostel has its own in-house bar. I'll try to tell you here when that's the case, but read the signs at check-in also.

As already mentioned, if it's a real hostel, it should have a kitchen for your use. That's nice, especially if there are no eateries nearby. Breakfast is less important, for me at least, though coffee and tea are certainly nice. So first thing I do upon arrival is stock up on food. If you wait too long, then there's no need. I tend to carry a few basics with me, so that's a start. Having a fridge is the most important thing. It's best to keep all your things in one bag and date and mark it as yours. Check the freebies bin if you're short of something. Don't take other people's food. Ask first. Most hostel people really ARE nice.

How This Book Works

How this book works is really simple. I've given you names, addresses, and phone numbers, everything but latitude and longitude, of the hostels included, so all you have to do is find the place. I advise to call ahead if you have no reservation. And I still advise booking ahead when possible, even when it's just two-three days away, so I've included website URL's, too. Many of those have contact forms within them. I've included e-mail addresses elsewhere. If you go from hostel to hostel, then you'll usually have Internet. Where this book comes in really handy is when that link is broken and you need to find a hostel when Internet is not readily available. Invariably somewhere the Internet will be down.

Of course it's the options that constitute the decision-making process in choosing a hostel, so in this guide all are listed for the following: Kitchen (or not), Breakfast (free or not or for purchase only), Wi-Fi (free or not or for purchase only), Private rooms (available or not), Lockers (available or not), and office hours. Most of this is common sense and easily understood, but a few categories may require explanation, e.g. private rooms. Hostels may be defined by their dorm beds, but for some of us, that's not optimal. I'm a light sleeper and don't appreciate being awoken in the middle of the night. Frequently I'll pay up to double to have my own room, and even then will usually come out ahead of a hotel. Nevertheless a place that has no dorms is not a hostel in my dictionary, so it's good to have both. But if you book a private room at a hostel, don't expect the same quality as a five-star hotel, or even a one-star. It's basic, but it's yours. And you might have to pay a pretty penny for that Wi-Fi elsewhere.

Lockers are fairly rare, actually, especially considering the security risk in an open dorm. Go figure. Thefts are rising. Costs are for comparison only and are something of an average, a price actually offered at a non-peak/non-slow time of year. There are always promotions and seasonal changes and varying specifications, so check around. A hostel-booking site might be cheaper than the hostel's own site. Some hostels have free WiFi; some charge; some have none, same with computers. Contact the hostel directly if the information here is insufficient. If you don't like using a credit card online, then contact the hostel and see if other arrangements are possible. Some require full payment in advance during special seasons. There are many hostel chains now, and I may not list them all in the same town. Check their website. Most of these hostels have websites or I won't list them. Information here can be outdated. Check their website or contact directly.

This book is intentionally intended to be part of a paradigm shift toward a new era in budget travel. If the old paradigm of the backpacker walking down the street with huge guidebook in hand trying to find budget accommodation is already out-of-date, then I think the one of booking them all in advance is not much better. There needs to be a balance of advance planning and spontaneity, guidebook and Internet. That's already the case, of course; I only propose to shift the balance toward less book and more Internet. This book is designed for that purpose. Not only do I hope to make hostelling better for backpackers, but I hope to see more hostels enter the mainstream, with better signage, better facilities, and ultimately more customers.

You might notice that addresses and phone numbers, everything but Internet addresses, are listed in several different ways. That's both accidental and intentional, accidental in that I tend to leave them as they're given to me, intentional in that you'll see them many ways, so this prepares you to adapt. With phone numbers generally "+" precedes an international number. With a cell phone, hold the "0" down and "+" will appear. That saves you from having to know codes *for international calling* (011, 001, etc.) in every country. That same number used within the country would usually drop the "+" and the 2-3 number code following it and add a "0" at the front. Compare them and you'll see. A picture is worth a thousand words. Skype will add the country code for you. I sometimes use a two-digit variation of the 24-hour clock here. For numbers larger than 12, subtract 12 for p.m. times. Now don't get all worried; go have some fun! The world is at your fingertips!

Key to Symbols: Here are some symbols, shorthand and abbreviations used in this book:

–$Bed = lowest price for a dorm bed that we can find for a typical day, for comparison only (they change with the season, with promotions, and with currency fluctuations)

–B'fast = Breakfast (free or not or for purchase only); typical for hostel (if anything) is a "continental breakfast," pastry & drink, cereal if you're lucky; don't expect eggs

–c.c. = credit card, OK meaning they're accepted, +/% indicating a surcharge for use; sometimes they are required as deposit, even if you're paying cash

–Recep = times when there should be someone to check you in. > means continuous working hours from one time to the next; /or // means they take a break in the middle (sometimes long); 24/7 means they never close, supposedly. I suggest advising & confirming late arrival. Don't press your luck

–HI, YHA, etc. = organizations of hostels which usually require membership; usually you can pay a small fee and gradually obtain membership

–central = hostel is centrally located in the city, generally a good thing for sight-seeing

–cash only = even if you reserved with plastic, they want cash for the balance

–luggage rm, luggage OK, etc = you can stash your luggage to pick up later, very handy

–Y.H. = Youth Hostel

–T = telephone (number); TF = toll-free (number); T/F = combined telephone/fax number

–lift = that's a bloody elevator, mate

–CBD = Central Business District = city center = 'downtown'

–*Jack1Free@ hypertravel.biz/* (for example) = my way of contracting e-mail addresses contained within domains, and shortening unwieldy too-long URL's regardless. The second half is the website address (add 'www' if necessary). The two together form the e-mail address (no spaces).

Note on other multi-language websites: you will also see a mini-UK flag on websites to indicate English language. That's the Union Jack, Jack. We Americans borrow their language, remember? *Tambien para el Espanol. Hay una bandera Espanola. Entiendes, Mendez? Sabes, Chavez?*

Introduction to the USA, Canada, and Mexico

First let's clarify our terms: I generally avoid using the term 'North America' because by it I'd mean the USA, Canada and Mexico, and many, if not most, experts would also include the Caribbean and/or Central America to the definition. Now the Caribbean is one thing, but Central America is a pretty well-defined term, and I've noticed that that term is not 'north.' And most of those people would also include Panama, which has no relationship at all to Central America, much less the North. And don't talk to me about tectonic plates, because Central America looks like somebody threw the plates on the floor and they shattered. By that measure there would be four to five continents in that region alone. No, for me these three countries define North America. Mexico is obviously the odd man out of this group, but maybe not as much as a quick glance might suggest.

Despite the Spanish language and Latino culture, Mexico in fact is odd man out of that group, too, with its heavily indigenous populace. And the roads and rivers between the US and Mexico run both ways, literally and figuratively. The interplay between us and the Mexicans is the stuff of myth and legend, not the least of which is the fact that more than a few US states used to be part of Mexico. And it started much earlier, too. Santa Fe was capital of the Spanish territory of Nuevo Mexico in 1620, when Pilgrims were still grubbing for worms at Plymouth Rock. The Spaniards were apparently much better at intermixing with the locals. *Orale guey.* I guess they left their wives at home; or maybe they just wanted some 'strange.' Whatever the logic, the back-story is solid. Mexico is not so much a Spanish culture as a culture of genetically-improved disease-resistant Aztecs come back to haunt us. I stand by my definitions. I sit on my burrito. I eat my tacos. South America has no tortillas. We do. Welcome to North America.

Part I: The United States

If you're American then you know the history well: the Mayflower, Boston Tea Party, Declaration of Independence, Revolutionary War, Constitution, War of 1812, Manifest Destiny, Texas and the Mexican War, slavery, War between the States, Reconstruction, Wild West, Robber Barons, World War I, Great Depression, World War II, Red Scare, Korea, Vietnam, Kuwait, Afghanistan, Iraq…

Sometimes it's hard to believe that the USA was once a revolutionary state, but we were, born and raised in the fires of revolt and shown to the rest of the world as an example of truth and justice and self-determination. Whatever we are now, we certainly aren't that, and our acceptance in the rest of the world is subject to certain limitations (keep that Canadian flag handy). Back home, of course, things are calmer, as long as you avoid certain neighborhoods. Being very much still a rural nation, inner-city areas tend to be neglected, usually to the detriment of us all, residents included. For the traveler, those areas are best avoided, or limited to daylight hours. Harlem should be on the itinerary of every traveler to New York City, after all. My grandmother was born there, after all. So should Farish Street in Jackson, Mississippi, one of the icons of my adolescence. Unfortunately there are no hostels there, closest one two hundred miles away.

Some of the best and coolest places in the USA still have no hostels. For my generation of counter-culture and back-to-nature, we looked for guidance and inspiration not to the financial and corporate power centers of New York, Los Angeles, Chicago, Dallas and Atlanta, but to the intellectual and cultural power centers of Berkeley, Ann Arbor, Boulder, Austin and Eugene. Today those places are still cool, but have few hostels — or none — while New York, LA, and the others are gradually joining the growing world trend of shared accommodations. That means that many international travelers will not even know that those cool places exist, much less be able to afford or access them. Most international travelers do not rent cars, nor should they have to.

Bottom line: Americans may not totally embrace the hostel concept until we've been able to remake it to our own specs, e.g. as cell-phones became smartphones and VCD's became DVD's. If that means combo shared/private pod-like spaces in larger comfier shared sleeping/living rooms, then I'm all for it.

1

Bunk-beds suck. I've seen or heard of this hybrid concept already in Japan, Canada, even Micronesia, as well as the USA, so this is not far-fetched. All we need is a semi-standardized pod design and marketing plan for it. If that pod is lockable, then it would obviate the need for lockers, too. Plus they would be more attractive. I'm working on it. One more thing about hostels and hotels and the bills you'll need to pay in the USA: (ALMOST) ALL HOSTELS CHARGE TAX IN ADDITION TO THE LISTED PRICE! Get used to it. Deal with it. Expect it. If you're European I know that this will piss you off, but just expect it. They generally run 10-20% of the bill, depending on the city. Can we just travel now?

1) Alaska

ANCHORAGE is Alaska's largest (and almost only) city, with a population of a quarter million, more if you count the surrounding suburbs. Whatever it lacks in urban amenities, it more than compensates for with spectacular natural surroundings, snow-capped peaks ringing a picturesque bay, even more spectacular than the far north. I was in the area in 2006 on a loop down from Fairbanks for the state fair in Palmer. Glaciers are nearby. It's far pricier than similar-sized cities down south. Hostels help.

Spenard Hostel International, 2845 W 42nd Ave, Anchorage, AK; *stay@ alaskahostel.org/*, T:+1(907)2485036; $27Bed, Pvt.room:Y, Kitchen:Y, B'fast:N, WiFi:Y, Locker:Y, Recep:9a/11p; Note: no alcohol, bikes, parking, luggage room, laundry, c.c. OK

Arctic Adventure Hostel, 337 W 33rd Ave, Anchorage, AK; *Info@ arcticadventurehostel.com/* , T:+1(907)5625700; $20Bed, Pvt.room:Y, Kitchen:Y, B'fast:N, WiFi:Y, Locker:N, Recep:9>10p; Note: parking, luggage room, laundry, tour desk, TV, books

Alaska Backpackers, 327 Eagle St, Anchorage, AK; *alaskabackpackers. com/*, T:+1(907)277.2770, *alaskabackpackers@gmail.com*; $25Bed, Pvt.room:Y,

Kitchen:Y, B'fast:N, WiFi:Y, Locker:N, Recep:24/7; Note: wh/chair OK, parking, luggage room, laundry, tour desk, wkly/monthly

Bent Prop Inn-Midtown, 3104 Eide St, Anchorage, AK; *midtown@ bentpropinn.com/*, T:+1(907)222.5220;

Bent Prop Inn-Downtown, 700 H St, Anchorage, AK; *downtown@ bentpropinn.com/*, T:+1(907)276.3635; $30Bed, Pvt.room:N, Kitchen:Y, B'fast:N, WiFi:Y, Locker:Y, Recep:24/7; Note: arpt trans, luggage room, laundry, maps, ATM, c.c.

Jason's Intl Youth Hostel, 3324 Eide St, Anchorage, AK; *jasonhostel.com/*, T:+1(907)562.0263, *jasonsih@aol.com*; $25Bed, Pvt.room:N, Kitchen:Y, B'fast:N, WiFi:Y, Locker:N, Recep:6a>2a; Note: resto/bar/club, parking, luggage room, laundry, tour desk, nr arpt

Alaska Youth Hostel, 2910 W. 31st Ave, Anchorage, AK; T:+1(907)310.2946;$25Bed, Pvt.room:Y, Kitchen:Y, B'fast:Y, WiFi:Y, Locker:N, Recep:ltd; Note: mansion, no alcohol, Jacuzzi/sauna/pool, café, wh/chair OK, nr arpt

Qupqugiaq Inn, 640 W. 36th Ave, Anchorage, AK; T:+1(907)563.5633, *qupq.com/*; $20Bed, Pvt.room:Y, Kitchen:Y, B'fast:$, WiFi:Y, Locker:N, Recep:ltd; Note: not central, resto, wh/chair OK, parking

FAIRBANKS is a city of over 30,000 and Alaska's second largest. At sixty-five degrees north latitude, it gets brutally cold in the winter (remember to plug in your car's engine-warmer at night) and surprisingly warm in the summer. You won't believe the size of veggies grown here. I saw the northern lights my first hour here in 2006.

Billie's Backpackers Hostel, 2895 Mack Blvd, Fairbanks, AK; *info@ alaskahostel.com/*; T:+1(907)479.2034; $28Bed, Pvt.room:N, Kitchen:N, B'fast:N, WiFi:Y, Locker:N, Recep:24/7; Note: bikes, minimart, parking, luggage room

Glacier House Hostel, 535 Glacier Ave, Fairbanks, AK; *hostelfairbanksalaska.com/*, T:+1(907)322.4946; $25Bed, Pvt.room:N, Kitchen:Y, B'fast:N, WiFi:Y, Locker:Y, Recep:24/7; Note: cash only, bikes, parking, luggage room, laundry $

3 Dog Night Hostel, 5972 Richardson Hwy, Salcha, Fairbanks, AK; *info@ 3dognighthostel.com/,* T:+1(907)590.8207; $30Bed, Pvt.room:Y, Kitchen:N, B'fast:N, WiFi:Y, Locker:N, Recep:24/7; Note: public bus 4xday, ½ hr>FBanks, bikes, parking, luggage rm, laundry

Chandalar Ranch, 5804 Chena Hot Springs Rd, Fairbanks, AK; *chandalarranchalaska.com/,*T:+1(907)488.8402; *kckoontz@alaska.net*; $40Bed, Pvt. room:Y, Kitchen:Y, B'fast:N, WiFi:Y, Locker:N, Recep:24/7; Note: arpt trans $, bush hostel, tour desk, Eskimo spoken J

TALKEETNA is a tiny town of less than 1000 a couple hours up the road from Anchorage toward Denali (Mt. McKinley). Founded about a hundred years ago, it doesn't feel like it's changed much since then. Outdoor activities are the ticket. I stopped through here in 2006 on my loop down from Fairbanks.

Talkeetna Alaska Hostel Intl, 22159 S I St, Talkeetna, AK; *talkeetnahostel. com/,* T:+1(907)733.4678, *talkeetnahostel@gmail.com*; $22Bed, Pvt.room:Y, Kitchen:Y, B'fast:N, WiFi:Y, Locker:N, Recep:10a>7p; Note: parking, camping, tea/coffee, walking distance to all

2) Arizona

FLAGSTAFF (*Dine*: 'Kinlani') is Arizona's mountain city, with a population over 60,000 and climbing. It sits at an elevation of almost 7000ft/2000mt in the country's largest Ponderosa Pine forest. It serves as a market town for the surrounding region and nearby Hopi and Dine (Navajo) Indian reservations. There is a ski resort at nearby San Francisco Peaks. It lies a couple hours north of Phoenix and is the biggest town between Albuquerque and Barstow on I-40 (and Hwy. 66). It also has the best coffee within a day's drive any direction. I lived here for ten to twenty years from 1987-2007, depending on how you count. It is famous for its observatories; Pluto was discovered here,

Grand Canyon Hostel, 19 S. San Francisco St, Flagstaff AZ; *info@ grandcanyonhostel.com/*, T:+1(928)779.9421; $24Bed, Pvt.room:N, Kitchen:Y, B'fast:Y, WiFi:Y, Locker:N, Recep:7a>12m; Note: shuttle, parking, tour desk, books

PHOENIX is Arizona's Gila (River) monster — city, that is — and one of the nation's largest, with a million and a half people in the city proper, and over four million in the 500sq.mi/1300sq.km land area. It is also the largest city in the US that is state capital, also. It sits smack on I-10 halfway between El Paso and Los Angeles. And if LA is the city that cars built, then Phoenix is the one that A/C built, that and swimming pools, sometimes considered a necessity in this part of the world. As many a tombstone reads, "It's a dry heat." On the positive side, downtown is making a comeback after many years of decline, and the airport is very centrally located. The Sonora Desert up around Carefree and Cave Creek is some of the most beautiful in the world (yep), Scottsdale is home to the rich and famous, while Tempe is the college town. Winter's nice.

HI Phoenix — Hostel/Cultural Center, 1026 N 9th St, Phoenix, AZ; *phxhostel.org/*, T:+1(602)254.9803; $25Bed, Pvt.room:Y, Kitchen:Y, B'fast:Y, WiFi:Y, Locker:Y, Recep:8a/8p; Note: arts dist, events, bikes, parking, laundry

Camel Backpackers, 1601 N 13th Ave, Phoenix, AZ; *camelbackpackers.com/*, T:+1(602)258.4143; $26Bed, Pvt.room:Y, Kitchen:Y, B'fast:Y, WiFi:Y, Locker:Y, Recep:24/7; Note: bikes, parking, laundry, luggage room, tour desk

WILLIAMS is a town of a few thousand in northern Arizona, and the other gateway — besides Flagstaff — to the Grand Canyon. The railroad to it runs from here. Like Flagstaff, it's cold, with an altitude almost 7000ft/2000mt.

The Grand Canyon Hotel, 145 W Rte 66, Williams, AZ; *thegrandcanyonhotel. com/*, T:+1(928)635.1419, *grandcanyonhotel@aol.com*; $40Bed, Pvt.room:Y, Kitchen:N, B'fast:N, WiFi:Y, Locker:N, Recep:6a/9p; Note: historic hotel, resto/bar, wh/chair OK, parking

3) California

FULLERTON is a town of some 135,000 in northern Orange County and part of the urban sprawl extending south from LA almost unbroken to San Diego (thank you, Camp Pendleton). It is the home of California State University.

HI Los Angeles/Fullerton, 1700 N. Harbor Blvd., Fullerton, CA; *fullerton@ hiusa.org/,* T:+1(714)738.3721; $24Bed, Pvt.room:N, Kitchen:Y, B'fast:Y, WiFi:Y, Locker:Y, Recep:ltd; Note: parking, tour desk, luggage room, laundry

HALF MOON BAY is an attractive town of some 11,000 situated between the inland forests and the deep blue sea. Located on the coastal highway between San Francisco and Santa Cruz, that coastline itself is especially beautiful.

HI Pigeon Pt Lighthouse, 210 Pigeon Pt Rd, Pescadero; T:+1(650)879.0633.

HI Point Montara Lighthouse, 16th St, Hwy 1, Montara, CA; *norcalhostels. org/montara,* T:+1(650)7287177; $27Bed, Pvt.room:Y, Kitchen:Y, B'fast:N, WiFi:Y, Locker:N, Recep:ltd; Note: wh/chair OK, parking, tour desk, luggage room

LOS ANGELES (inc. Hollywood, Venice, Inglewood, Santa Monica, Hermosa Beach) is one of the largest cities in the world — and second in the US after New York — with almost 18 million in the Greater LA area, though less than four million in the city proper, "100 suburbs in search of a city." This is uniquely LA and peculiar to the auto-culture that spawned it, sprawling out over 500 sq.mi/1300sq.km. Besides the beaches and auto-culture, LA is probably best known for the fruit of its Hollywood fantasy factory, a movie industry that brings the streets (and highways) of LA to TV screens all around the world in the form of cheap entertainment. This all started some 240 years ago as a pueblo on the Serra mission trail, with a grand total of 650 residents after 50 years, *zzzleeepy...*

By 1900 the population was over 100,000. It hosted Olympics in 1932 and 1984. Landmarks and tourist destinations include Griffith Observatory, Getty Center, Los Angeles County Museum of Art, Grauman's Chinese Theatre, the Hollywood Sign, Hollywood Boulevard, the Capitol Records Building, Hollywood Bowl, Watts Towers, Staples Center, Dodger

Stadium, and Olvera Street. There's now a subway/light rail network that makes LA a much nicer place than it used to be, just like that other city of angels way out east, or west, or north, □□ □□□□□□□□□□□,say what?

USA Hostels-Hollywood, 1624 Schrader Bl, Hollywood, CA; *hollywood@ usahostels.com/*, TF:+1(800)524.6783; $37Bed, Kitchen:Y, B'fast:Y, WiFi:Y, Pvt. room:N, Locker:Y, Recep:ltd; Note: arpt trans, laundry, luggage rm, parking, tour desk, c.c. OK, a/c

Banana Bungalow West Hollywood, 603 N Fairfax Ave, W. Hollywood, CA; *westhollywood@ bananabungalowus.com/*, T:+1(323)655.2002

Banana Bungalow Hollywood, 5920 Hollywood Bl, Hollywood, CA; *hollywood@ bananabungalowus.com/*, TF:1(877)977.5077; $30Bed, Kitchen:Y, B'fast:Y, WiFi:Y, Pvt.room:N, Locker:Y, Recep:24/7; Note: gym, bikes, arpt trans, laundry, luggage rm, parking, tour desk, party

Duo Hostel, 886 Crenshaw Blvd, Los Angeles, CA; *duohousing.com/*, T+1(310)715.9194; $22Bed, Kitchen:Y, B'fast:N, WiFi:N, Pvt.room:N, Locker:Y, Recep:24/7; Note: laundry, luggage rm, parking, tour desk, c.c. ONLY, Korea-town

Orange Drive Hostel, 1764 N Orange Dr, Los Angeles, CA; *info@ orangedrivehostel.com/*, T:+1(323)850.0350; $34Bed, Kitchen:Y, B'fast:Y, WiFi:Y, Pvt.room:Y, Locker:$, Recep:7a>12m; Note: trad house, luggage room, terrace, parking, TV, fireplace, piano

Surf City Hostel, 26 Pier Ave, Hermosa Beach, CA; *info@ surfcityhostel. com/*, T:1+(310)798.2323; $30Bed, Kitchen:Y, B'fast:Y, WiFi:Y, Pvt.room:N, Locker:Y, Recep:24/7; Note: resto/club, bikes, laundry, luggage rm, parking, tour desk, nr beach

Backpackers Paradise (Adventurer Hostel), 4200 W Century Bl, Inglewood; *backpackersparadise.com/*, T:+1(310)419.0999, *laadventurerhtl@yahoo.com*;$15Bed, Kitchen:N, B'fast:N, WiFi:Y, Pvt.room:Y, Locker:Y, Recep:24/7; Note: free arpt p-u, pool, resto/bar, wheelchair OK, laundry, luggage room

Samesun Venice Beach, 25 Windward Ave, Venice, CA; *samesun. com/*, TF:+1(877)972.6378, $28Bed, Kitchen:Y, B'fast:N, WiFi:Y, Pvt.room:Y, Locker:Y, Recep:24/7; Note: arpt trans, bikes, luggage rm, bar, tour desk, tea/ coffee, c.c. OK, pubs

Hollywood YH, 6820 Hollywood Bl, Los Angeles, CA; *ushostel.com/*, T:+1(323)463.2770; $20Bed, Kitchen:Y, B'fast:N, WiFi:Y, Pvt.room:Y, Locker:Y, Recep:24/7; Note: bar, cash only.ATM, laundry, luggage room, TV, billiards, party

Venice Beach Hostel (Planet Venice), 1515 Pacific Ave, Venice, CA; *info@ planetvenice.com/*, T:+1(310)452.3052; $40Bed, Kitchen:Y, B'fast:Y, WiFi:Y, Pvt. room:Y, Locker:Y, Recep:24/7; Note: minimart, laundry, luggage rm, billiards, tour desk

Stay On Main, 636 S Main St, Los Angeles, CA; *stayonmain.com/* , T:+1(213)213.7829; $35Bed, Kitchen:N, B'fast:Y, WiFi:Y, Pvt.room:Y, Locker:Y, Recep:24/7; Note: downtown, café lift, laundry, luggage rm, ATM, tour desk

The Podshare, 1617 Cosmo St, Los Angeles, CA; *thepodshare.com/*, T:+1(213)973.7741; $40Bed, Kitchen:Y, B'fast:N, WiFi:Y, Pvt.room:Y, Locker:Y, Recep:24/7; Note: cash only, laundry, parking, custom-built futuristic bunks

THE Venice Beach Hostel, 716 Washington Bl, Venice, CA; *venicebeachhostel.com/*, T:1(310)301.3983, *venicebeachhostel@yahoo.com*; $25Bed, Kitchen:Y, B'fast:Y, WiFi:Y, Pvt.room:Y, Locker:Y, Recep:ltd; Note: free arpt p-u, bikes, billiards, laundry, luggage room

HI-Los Angeles/Santa Monica, 1436 Second St, Santa Monica, CA; T:+1(310)393.9913, *reserve@ HILosAngeles.org/*; $35Bed, Pvt.room:N, Kitchen:Y, B'fast:Y, WiFi:Y, Locker:Y, Recep:24/7; Note: wh/chair OK, billiards, bikes, lift, tour desk

MoonPad LA, 1700 E 4th Street #203, Los Angeles, CA

MoonPad, 125 S. Boyle Ave, Los Angeles, CA; *themoonpad.com/*; T:+1(310)426.8536, *manager@themoonbridge.com*; $20Bed, Pvt.room:N, Kitchen:Y, B'fast:Y, WiFi:Y, Locker:Y, Recep:24/7; Note: parking, luggage room, c.c. OK

MARIN COUNTY is that area directly to the north of San Francisco beyond the Golden Gate Bridge, with beaches on both the bay and the ocean sides. And, if San Francisco defines American urban hipness, Marin County pretty well defines its suburban counterpart. Though it may be mostly populated by bedroom communities and big-city commuters, there is a human and geographical diversity that defies easy definition.

Part I: The United States

HI Point Reyes, 1390 Limantour Spit Rd, Point Reyes, CA; +1(415)663.8811

HI Marin Headlands, Fort Barry Building 941, Sausalito, CA; *norcalhostels. org/marin/*, T:+1(415)3312777; $25Bed, Pvt.room:Y, Kitchen:Y, B'fast:N, WiFi:Y, Locker:Y, Recep:ltd; Note: laundry, parking, historic bldg, wh/chair OK, luggage room

MONTEREY is a city of almost 28,000, but with a history that is vastly more important than that. It was founded in 1770 by Padre Junipero Serra himself, and served as the capital of California under Spain, then Mexico, before the *gabachos* took over right before the Gold Rush. The bay is beautiful.

HI Monterey Hostel, 778 Hawthorne St, Monterey, CA; *info@ montereyhostel.org*; T:+1(831)649.0375; $23Bed, Pvt.room:N, Kitchen:N, B'fast:Y, WiFi:Y, Locker:Y, Recep:8a>10p; Note: wh/chair OK, bikes, parking, tour desk, luggage room, non party, central

SACRAMENTO is the capital of California and its sixth-largest city, with almost 500K, over four times that in the metro area. It grew up in the Gold Rush of 1849 and that event offers most of the modern-day tourist attractions — Sutter's Fort and Old Sacramento. It is well-connected, at the junction of I-5 and I-40, and a hub for Amtrak and Greyhound.

HI Sacramento, 925 H St, Sacramento, CA; *norcalhostels.org/sac*, T:+1(916)443.1691; $29Bed, Pvt.room:Y, Kitchen:Y, B'fast:Y, WiFi:Y, Locker:Y, Recep:24/7; Note: Vic mansion, central, wh/chair OK, parking, luggage room, laundry

SAN DIEGO is the 2nd largest city in California, with almost a million and a half in the city proper, and twice that in the metro area, which includes Tijuana across the Mexican border. *Hola!* Mission San Diego and *presidio* (fort) were founded in 1769 as the anchor tenant on the Serra trail and soon had the largest native population in the north (of Baja). They are both now national historic sites and comprise the area north of downtown known as Old Town. New Town — now downtown — proved more popular with its seaside location. San Diego soon became a navy base and "tuna capital of the world."

After a long decline, downtown and especially the Gaslamp Quarter have been refurbished and is an entertainment district. That and beaches, year-round sunshine and proximity to Mexico have made San Diego quite the tourist draw, but it's not the bargain it used to be, too bad. Hostels help. Favorite attractions are Balboa Park, San Diego Zoo, Safari Park, and SeaWorld San Diego. Events and festivals include Comic-Con, San Diego Pride, the San Diego Black Film Festival, and Street Scene Music Festival. Also, microbreweries are well-known here, so there are "beer tours" and the annual San Diego Beer Week in November. San Diego has one of the few centrally-located airports in the world, barely a 15-minute ride on the 992 bus. Bus and train are within walking distance downtown. There's light-rail, too, the Tijuana trolley. I was here for the first time back in 1992, before they remodeled the Gaslamp Quarter. I called it.

Intl Travelers House, 1658 Front St, San Diego, CA; *info@ sdtravelershouse. com/*, T:+1(619)228.9234; $26Bed, Pvt.room:N, Kitchen:Y, B'fast:Y, WiFi:Y, Locker:Y, Recep:24/7; Note: Little Italy, shuttle, minimart, tour desk, luggage room, laundry, party

Lucky D's Hostel, 615-8th Ave, San Diego, CA; *info@ luckydshostel.com/*, T:+1(619)595.0000; $25Bed, Pvt.room:Y, Kitchen:N, B'fast:Y, WiFi:Y, Locker:Y, Recep:24/7; Note: bar, bikes, luggage room, c.c. OK, free meals, Gaslamp Qtr

HI San Diego-Downtown, 521 Market St, San Diego, CA; *downtown@ sandiegohostels.org*, T:+1(619)525.1531

HI San Diego-Point Loma, 3790 Udall St, San Diego, CA; *sandiegohostels. org/*, T:+1(619)223.4778; $23Bed, Pvt.room:Y, Kitchen:Y, B'fast:Y, WiFi:N, Locker:Y, Recep:8a>10p; Note: wh/chair OK, parking, tour desk, luggage room, laundry, Ocean Beach

RK Hostel, 642 W Hawthorn St, San Diego, CA; *rkhostel.com/*, T:+1(619)564.6914; $25Bed, Pvt.room:Y, Kitchen:Y, B'fast:Y, WiFi:Y, Locker:N, Recep:24/7; Note: Little Italy, nr arpt, tour desk, luggage room, laundry

California Dreams Backpacker's Hostel, 743-7 Emerald St, San Diego, CA; *californiadreamshostel@hotmail.com*, T:+1(858)246.7101, *californiadreamshostel. com/*; $20Bed, Pvt.room:Y, Kitchen:N, B'fast:Y, WiFi:Y, Locker:Y, Recep:24/7; Note: wn/chair OK, parking, tour desk, c.c. OK, near beach

Banana Bungalow San Diego, 707 Reed Ave, San Diego, CA; T:+1(858)273.3060, *Info@ bananabungalowsandiego.com*; $37Bed, Pvt.room:N,

Kitchen:N, B'fast:Y, WiFi:Y, Locker:$, Recep:24/7; Note: parking, laundry, beer coolers, boogie boards, beach, party

Ocean Beach Intl Hostel, 4961 Newport Ave, San Diego, CA; *californiahostel. com/*, T:+1(619)223.7873, *obihostel@aol.com*; $25Bed, Pvt.room:Y, Kitchen:Y, B'fast:Y, WiFi:Y, Locker:Y, Recep:ltd; Note: arpt trans, parking, tour desk, luggage room, laundry, meals

AAE San Diego Travel Inn, 425 W Main St, San Diego; T:+1(304)268.8981

AAE Hostel San Diego, 500 W Broadway, San Diego, CA; T:+1(619)234.5252, *500westhotel.aaeworldhotels.com/*; $28Bed, Pvt.room:Y, Kitchen:Y, B'fast:N, WiFi:Y, Locker:Y, Recep:24/7; Note: café, gym, wh/chair OK, lift, tour desk, minimart, basic

USA Hostels San Diego, 726-5th Ave, San Diego, CA; *sandiego@ usahostels. com/*, T:+1(619)232.3100; $29Bed, Pvt.room:Y, Kitchen:Y, B'fast:Y, WiFi:Y, Locker:Y, Recep:24/7; Note: Gaslamp dist, tour desk, luggage room, laundry, activities

Hostel on 3rd, 542-3rd Ave, San Diego, CA; *hostelon3rd.com/*, T:+1(619)595.1440, *hostelon3rd@gmail.com*; $25Bed, Pvt.room:Y, Kitchen:Y, B'fast:Y, WiFi:Y, Locker:Y, Recep:ltd; Note: Gaslamp dist, nightclub, billiards, laundry, tour desk

St.Christopher Intl YH, 2420 India St, San Diego, CA; *St.ChristopherIYH_ SD@yahoo.com*, T:+1(619)607.0086; (see FB Page), $23Bed, Pvt.room:N, Kitchen:Y, B'fast:Y, WiFi:Y, Locker:N, Recep:ltd; Note: foreign/non-CA guests, laundry, pancakes

SAN FRANCISCO is one of the most beautiful cities in the USA: our Rio, our Capetown, our Rome. It is also a city of 800,000 in a Bay Area of more than seven million, fourth largest in the state by itself, draped over the hills like silk, sprouting architecture like porcelain. It was founded in 1776 and rocketed up in growth with the Gold Rush of 1849. Then an earthquake struck in 1906 and fires broke out that raged for days, destroying most of the city. It became a counterculture magnet with the Beat Generation and hippies in the 1950's and 60's. It became even more of a haven of LGBT activism a decade or so later, especially when Harvey Milk was elected councilman and subsequently assassinated along with Mayor George Moscone in 1978.

After all the port activity, dot-com start-ups, and financial wheelings and dealings, San Fran is at its best just making people feel good, and that means tourism. Best of all, you can see most of it by walking. That includes the districts of North Beach, Chinatown, the Embarcadero, Fisherman's Wharf, Union Square, Noe Valley, the Castro District, the Financial District, the Mission District, the Sunset District, Nob Hill, South of Market, Golden Gate Park, and Haight-Ashbury, all totally unique and totally welcoming. Museums include the San Francisco Museum of Modern Art, the de Young Museum, the Asian Art Museum, the California Academy of Sciences, the Palace of Fine Arts, and the Exploratorium, an interactive science museum. Top draw is Golden Gate Bridge. This is one of my favorite places in the world. No, I'm not gay.

USA Hostels San Francisco, 711 Post St, San Francisco, CA; *sanfrancisco@ usahostels.com/*, T:+1(415)440.5600; $46Bed, Pvt.room:Y, Kitchen:Y, B'fast:Y, WiFi:Y, Locker:Y, Recep:24/7; Note: arpt trans, tour desk, luggage room, laundry, meals, downtown

Green Tortoise, 494 Broadway St, San Francisco, CA; *greentortoise.com/*, T:+1(415)834.1000; $33Bed, Pvt.room:N, Kitchen:Y, B'fast:Y, WiFi:Y, Locker:Y, Recep:24/7; Note: North Beach, arpt trans, party, luggage room, laundry, billiards

Adelaide Hostel, 5 Isadora Duncan Ln, San Francisco, CA; *info@ adelaidehostel.com/*, T:+1(415)359.1915; $35Bed, Pvt.room:Y, Kitchen:Y, B'fast:Y, WiFi:Y, Locker:Y, Recep:24/7; Note: bikes, arpt trans, tour desk, luggage room, laundry, meals, 2 locations

Orange Village Hostel, 411 O'Farrell St, San Francisco, CA; *orangevillagehostel.com/*, T:+1(415)409.4000; $27Bed, Pvt.room:Y, Kitchen:Y, B'fast:Y, WiFi:Y, Locker:Y, Recep:24/7; Note: parking, lift, arpt trans, tour desk, luggage room, laundry, dntn, basic

HI- San Francisco City Center, 685 Ellis St, San Francisco, CA; *sfhostels. com/city-center/*, T:+1(415)474.5721

HI- San Francisco Fishermans-Wharf, 240 Fort Mason, San Francisco, CA; *sfhostels.com/fishermans-wharf*, T:+1(415)771.7277;

HI- San Francisco Downtown, 312 Mason St, San Francisco, CA; *sfhostels. com/downtown/*; T:+1(415)788.5604; $42Bed, Pvt.room:Y, Kitchen:Y, B'fast:Y,

WiFi:Y, Locker:Y, Recep:24/7; Note: wh/chair OK, lift, luggage room, activities: pub crawls, etc

AAE- SF European Hostel, 761 Minna St, San Francisco, CA; *sfhostel. aaeworldhotels.com/*, T:+1(304)268.8981; $20Bed, Pvt.room:Y, Kitchen:Y, B'fast:Y, WiFi:Y, Locker:Y, Recep:24/7; Note: SOMA area, bikes, tour desk, luggage room, laundry, c.c. OK, basic

Encore Express Hotel, 1353 Bush St, San Francisco CA; T:+1(415)816.6207, *encoreexpresshotel.com/*; $25Bed, Pvt.room:Y, Kitchen:Y, B'fast:N, WiFi:Y, Locker:Y, Recep:10a>11p; Note: luggage room, laundry, Union Sq, loud music

San Francisco Intl Hostel, 140 Mason St, San Francisco, CA; *sanfranhostel. com/*, T:1(888)919.0140; $29Bed, Pvt.room:N, Kitchen:N, B'fast:Y, WiFi:Y, Locker:Y, Recep:24/7; Note: café/bar, pool, bikes, wh/chair OK, luggage room, laundry, parking

Union Square Backpacker's Hostel, 70 Derby St, San Francisco, CA; *mybackpackershostel.com/*, T:+1(415)775.7506; $21Bed, Pvt.room:Y, Kitchen:Y, B'fast:Y, WiFi:Y, Locker:Y, Recep:8a>11p; Note: central, bikes, tour desk, luggage room, laundry, TV, basic

Amsterdam Hostel, 749 Taylor St, San Francisco, CA; *amsterdamhostel. org/*, T:+1(304)268.8981, *amsterdamsf@aol.com*; $21Bed, Pvt.room:Y, Kitchen:Y, B'fast:Y, WiFi:Y, Locker:N, Recep:24/7: Note: wh/chair OK, tour desk, luggage room, parking, c.c. OK, a/c, laundry

SAN LUIS OBISPO is a small pleasant city of 45K located on Hwy. 101 between San Francisco and Los Angeles, route of the old Camino Real. The first Mo-Tel was opened here. There is a film festival. Bubblegum Alley is where people have been sticking bubblegum since 1960. No comment.

HI Hostel Obispo, 1617 Santa Rosa St, San Luis Obispo, CA; *reservations@ hostelobispo.com/*, T:+1(805)544.4678; $26Bed, Pvt.room:N, Kitchen:Y, B'fast:N, WiFi:Y, Locker:N, Recep:ltd; Note: wh/chair OK, bikes, parking, laundry, central

SANTA ANA is part of the greater Los Angeles metropolitan area, and the second-largest city in Orange County, with over 300,000 residents.

Orange Mango Garden Hostel, 2609 Patti Lane, Santa Ana, CA; *facebook. com/omghostel*, T:+1(949)307.9052, *omghostel@gmail.com*; $24Bed, Pvt.room:N, Kitchen:Y, B'fast:N, WiFi:Y, Locker:Y, Recep:7a>11p; Note: min 3N, bikes, luggage room, cash only

SANTA BARBARA is a pleasant little city of almost 90,000 located along the Pacific coast an hour or two up from LA, depending on local traffic conditions. With a history dating back to the Spanish and Mexican eras, its fate was sealed — and its population quickly doubled — when the *gabachos* took over. Still the Mexican influence remains in the architecture, food and (relatively) laid-back ambience of the place. The mission anchors it, the Presidio is a landmark, and the annual Fiesta celebrates it, just as the Beach Music and Arts Festival celebrates its contemporary culture. There is also a film festival and a major annual arts and crafts fair.

AAE Santa Barbara, 111 N. Milpas, G-H bus/Amtrak, Sta. Barbara; *santabarbara.aaeworldhotels.com/*, T:+1(805)308.1240; $30Bed, Pvt.room:Y, Kitchen:Y, B'fast:Y, WiFi:Y, Locker:Y, Recep:ltd; Note: parking, luggage room, tea/coffee, c.c. OK, not central, walk>beach

Santa Barbara Tourist Hostel, 134 Chapala St, Santa Barbara CA; *info@ sbhostel.com/*, T:+1(805)963.0154; $30Bed, Pvt.room:Y, Kitchen:Y, B'fast:Y, WiFi:Y, Locker:Y, Recep:8a>10p; Note: parking, luggage room, tour desk, walk>beach

YOSEMITE NATIONAL PARK is one of the key links in the National Park System, covering 761,268acres/3080sq.km in east-central California. It is 95% wilderness, with elevations ranging from 2000>13,000ft/650>4000mt. It is a UNESCO designated world heritage site. If you're short of time and have places to go, following Hwy. 120 through the park east to west or vice-versa is not bad. That's what I did.

Yosemite Bug Rustic Mt. Resort, 6979 Ca. Hwy 140, Midpines, CA; *yosemitebug.com/*, T:+1(209)966.6666, *bughost@yosemitebug.com*; $23Bed, Pvt. room:N, Kitchen:Y, B'fast:N, WiFi:Y, Locker:Y, Recep:ltd; Note: resto/bar, wh/chair OK, parking, luggage rm, laundry, YARTS bus

Oso Hostel, Groveland, Yosemite National Park, CA; *manager@ osohostel. com/*, T:+1(209)962.0365; $35Bed, Pvt.room:Y, Kitchen:Y, B'fast:$, WiFi:Y, Locker:N, Recep:24/7; Note: bar, bikes, parking, luggage rm, laundry

4) Colorado

ASPEN is the Rocky Mountain ski resort *par excellence*, world-renowned and celebrity-studded. It has more feet of elevation than it does (permanent) residents, 8000ft/2400mt to less than 7000 people. Once a Mecca of the counterculture, it now has the most expensive real estate in the US. I guess that's why I've never gone. Hostels help.

St. Moritz Lodge, 334 W Hyman Ave, Aspen, CO; *info@ stmoritzlodge. com/*, T:+1(970)925.3220; $33Bed, Pvt.room:Y, Kitchen:N, B'fast:Y, WiFi:Y, Locker:N, Recep:ltd; Note: pool, hot tub, laundry, parking, central

BRECKENRIDGE is high up in the Rocky Mountains at an elevation of 9600ft/3000mt. It has a population of almost 5000 including many part-timers. It's a ski town. Summertime is for hiking and lake activities. There is a film festival.

Fireside Inn, 114 N French St, Breckenridge, CO; *firesideinn.com/*, T:+1(970)453.6456, *fireside@colorado.net*; $30Bed, Pvt.room:Y, Kitchen:Y, B'fast:$, WiFi:Y, Locker:N, Recep:4p>8p; Note: arpt trans, parking, luggage room, hot tub, games, fax, c.c. OK

DENVER is Colorado's largest city and capital, and the largest of the Rocky Mountain region. It sits a mile—5280ft/1600mt—above sea level along the jagged line where the Great Plains meet the Rocky Mountains. The Continental Divide is a short drive away. It also sits at the intersection of highways I-25 and I-70; excursions into the nearby mountains are fun, as are excursions to the nearby college town of Boulder. A river runs through it. I lived in the *La Raza barrio* for a while back in the mid-70's, *chevere*.

AAE 11th Ave Hostel, 1112 Broadway, Greyhound/Amtrak Dntn, Denver; *denver.aaeworldhotels.com/*, T:+1(304)268.8981; $21Bed, Kitchen:Y, B'fast:N, WiFi:Y, Pvt.room:Y, Locker:Y, Recep:24/7; Note: resto, TV, downtown, common room

Denver Intl Hostel, 630 E. 16th Ave, Denver, CO; *youthhostels.com/denver/*, T:+1(303)832.9996, *denverhostel@gmail.com*; $17Bed, Pvt.room:Y, Kitchen:Y,

B'fast:N, WiFi:Y, Locker:N, Recep:8a//10p; Note: midday lockout, very basic, cash only, central, TV

FRASER is a town of 900 at an elevation of 8550ft/2600mt in northern Colorado. The ski Mecca (or is it Medina?) of Winter Park is nearby.

The Rocky Mountain Chalet, 15 County Rd 72, Fraser, CO; *admin@ therockymountainchalet.com/*, T:+1(970)726.8256; $28Bed, Pvt.room:N, Kitchen:Y, B'fast:N, WiFi:Y, Locker:Y, Recep:ltd; Note: shuttle, wh/chair OK, coffee/tea, laundry, nr WinterPark/Amtrak

GLENWOOD SPRINGS is a town of almost 10,000 in the heart of the Colorado Rockies and a regular daily stop of Amtrak's California Zephyr from Chicago to Oakland and vice-versa, along routes that can be seen no other way. Outdoor and nature-oriented activities are the ticket here. There are bus connections to Aspen and elsewhere.

Glenwood Springs Hostel, 1021 Grand Ave, Glenwood Springs, CO; *gshostel@ hostelcolorado.com/*, T:+1(970)945.8545; $20Bed, Pvt.room:Y, Kitchen:N, B'fast:N, WiFi:N, Locker:N, Recep:8a/10p; Note: pool, parking, tour desk, midday lockout, basic

5) District of Columbia

WASHINGTON, DC ("the District," "D.C.") refers to the country's capital district, of course (NOT the Pac NW state), that 68.3sq.mi/177sq.km parcel of land wedged between Maryland and Virginia that holds more than 600,000 people (1M+ during work hours, almost 6M in the metro area) and tries to rule a world in fits and starts. This is a purpose-built entity, of course, mandated by Congress in 1790 and holding its first Congressional session in 1800. The design is patterned after some of the best of European cities.

Height restrictions have led to sprawl and housing shortages in the city core. The Brits burned and gutted the place in 1814, and blacks rioted after Martin Luther King's assassination in 1968, but other than that, there were few major disasters... until 11 Sept. 2001, when American Airlines flight #77 was piloted directly into the Pentagon, headquarters of the Department of Defense.

The city is a tourist's wet dream, though, with more tourist sites than the rest of the country put together, e.g. the White House; the Washington National Cathedral; the Thomas Jefferson Memorial; the United States Capitol; the Lincoln Memorial; and the Vietnam Veterans Memorial, combining neoclassical, Georgian, gothic, and modern architectural styles. Having been carved out of the old South, and a refuge for freed slaves, blacks form the majority of the population in the core. Poverty is also higher than elsewhere in the country, and crime is high. Government is the big employer, of course, and there are many international organizations, such as the UN, World Bank, the International Monetary Fund (IMF), the Organization of American States, the Inter-American Development Bank, and the Pan American Health Organization. Museums include the Smithsonian American Art Museum, the National Portrait Gallery, and the Renwick Gallery. There is a subway, bus and rail links, and several airports.

Duo Housing DC, 1223-11th St. NW, Washington DC; *duohousing.com/*, T:+1(202)640.3755; $30Bed, Pvt.room:N, Kitchen:Y, B'fast:N, WiFi:Y, Locker:Y, Recep:24/7; Note: books, maps, tour desk, luggage room, central;

Downtown Washington Hostel, 506-H St NE, Washington DC; *downtownwashingtonhostel.com/*, T:+1(202)370.6390; $30Bed, Pvt.room:N, Kitchen:Y, B'fast:Y, WiFi:Y, Locker:Y, Recep:24/7; Note: terrace, laundry, tour desk, luggage room, 'King of H St', spaghetti

Capital View, 301-I St NW, Washington DC; T:+1(202)450.3450

DC Lofty Convention Center, 1333-11th St NW, Washington, DC; *contact@ capitalhostels.com/*, T:+1(202)506.7106; $26Bed, Pvt.room:Y, Kitchen:Y, B'fast:N, WiFi:Y, Locker:Y, Recep:10a>10p; Note: luggage room, laundry, parking, c.c. OK, books, a/c

HI Washington DC, 1009-11th St NW, Washington, DC; T:+1(202)737.2333, *reserve@ hiwashingtondc.org/*, $29Bed, Pvt.room:Y, Kitchen:Y, B'fast:Y, WiFi:Y, Locker:Y, Recep:24/7; Note: lift, billiards, laundry, tour desk, luggage room, tea/coffee, central

Washington Intl Student Center, 2451-18ᵗʰ St NW, Washington, DC; *dchostel.com/*, T:+1(202)667.7681, *dcstudentcenter@gmail.com*; $28Bed, Pvt. room:Y, Kitchen:Y, B'fast:Y, WiFi:Y, Locker:Y, Recep:8a>11p; Note: bus/train pickup, swimming pool, luggage room, a/c

Hilltop Hostel, 300 Carroll St NW, Washington, DC; *info@ hosteldc.com/*, T:+1(202)291.9591; $24Bed, Pvt.room:N, Kitchen:Y, B'fast:N, WiFi:Y, Locker:Y, Recep:ltd; Note: trad house, cash only, minimart, billiards, laundry, luggage room

The Allen Lee Hotel, 2224-F St NW, Washington, DC; *information@ theallenleehotel.com/*, T:+1(202)331.1224; $45Bed, Pvt.room:Y, Kitchen:Y, B'fast:Y, WiFi:Y, Locker:N, Recep:24/7; Note: Foggy Bottom area, lift, luggage room, a/c, nr subway, basic

Intl House Of Washington (United Tel), 1110-6ᵗʰ St NW, Washington, DC; *budgethotelswashingtondc.com/*, T:+1(518)203.2086, *uti@bww.com*; $36Bed, Pvt. room:N, Kitchen:Y, B'fast:Y, WiFi:Y, Locker:Y, Recep:8a>11p; Note: laundry, parking, luggage room, tea/coffee

Capitol City Hostel, 2411 Benning Rd NE, Washington, DC; *cheapesthostel. com/*, T:+1(202)387.1328, *good4uandus@hotmail.com*; $25Bed, Pvt.room:N, Kitchen:N, B'fast:Y, WiFi:Y, Locker:N, Recep:ltd; Note: parking, a/c, no-smoke, nr bus station

Canal Inn Georgetown, 1061-31ˢᵗ St NW, Washington DC; *canalinnhotel.com/*, T:+1(202)333.1525; $50Bed, Pvt.room:Y, Kitchen:Y, B'fast:Y, WiFi:Y, Locker:Y, Recep:ltd; Note: arpt trans, luggage room, laundry, TV, a/c, c.c. OK

Capital Comfort Hostel, 1610-7ᵗʰ St NW, Washington DC; *steve@ capitalcomforthostel.com/*, T:1(877)889.6499; $18Bed, Pvt.room:N, Kitchen:Y, B'fast:N, WiFi:Y, Locker:N, Recep:ltd; Note: arpt trans, lift, laundry, a/c, central, basic

Diplomatic Stay, 4907-14ᵗʰ St, Northwest, Washington DC; *diplomaticstay@ gmail.com*, T:+1(202)538.3503, *facebook.com/DiplomaticStay/*; $35Bed, Pvt. room:Y, Kitchen:Y, B'fast:N, WiFi:Y, Locker:Y, Recep:11a>10p; Note: 5N max, hot tub, tennis, bikes, forex, laundry, luggage room, c.c. OK

6) Florida

EVERGLADES is a town of 500 in southern Florida and gateway to the national park of the same name, the USA's most significant and vast area of wetlands.

Everglades Hostel, 20 SW 2nd Ave, Florida City, FL; *evergladeshostel.com/*, T+1(305)248.1122, *gladeshostel@hotmail.com*; $20Bed, Pvt.room:N, Kitchen:Y, B'fast:Y, WiFi:Y, Locker:Y, Recep:24/7; Note: pool, café, minimart, luggage rm, laundry, c.c. OK, unique tours

FORT LAUDERDALE is a city of only a couple hundred thou, but part of the mega-metropolis of south Florida that includes Miami and tops five million. Tourism is the main business. For many years that meant college students on spring break; now it means yachts and LGBT tourists. The nightlife is legendary.

The Deauville Hotel, 2916 N Ocean Bl, Ft Lauderdale, FL; *thedeauvillehotel. com/*, T:+1(954)568.5000, *thehoteldeauville@yahoo.com*; $30Bed, Pvt.room:Y, Kitchen:Y, B'fast:N, WiFi:Y, Locker:Y, Recep:12n>11p; Note: bikes, pool, parking, gym

Bridge at Cordova, 1441 Cordova Rd, Ft Lauderdale, FL; *bridgeatcordova. com/*, T:+1(954)523.7090, *thebridgebedandbreakfast@gmail.com*; $30Bed, Pvt. room:Y, Kitchen:Y, B'fast:Y, WiFi:Y, Locker:Y, Recep:24/7; Note: pool, bikes, wh/chair OK, gym, luggage room, laundry, tour desk

Hollywood Beach Hostel, 320 Arizona St, Ft Lauderdale, FL; *hollywoodbeachhostel.com/*, T:+1(954)391.9448, *pamela.garcia@southbeachgroup. com*; $22Bed, Pvt.room:Y, Kitchen:Y, B'fast:Y, WiFi:Y, Locker:Y, Recep:8a>11p; Note: restos, bikes, wh/chair OK, parking, a/c, not central

KEY WEST (*Cayo Hueso*) is the southernmost point physically connected to the continental US, a part of the collection of sand and salt ponds that define the Florida 'keys' (*cayos*). The name derives from an Anglicization of the word '*hueso*', or 'bone.'

Key West YH & Sea Shell Motel, 718 South St, Key West, FL; *kwssm. com/*, T:+1(305)296.5719, *kwssm@bellsouth.net*; $49Bed, Pvt.room:N, Kitchen:Y,

B'fast:N, WiFi:Y, Locker:Y, Recep:ltd; Note: 4 blks>point, bikes, laundry, a/c, c.c. OK, basic

MIAMI is city of 400,000, with more than 5.5 million in the greater metropolitan area, of which it is the center. With a Spanish-speaking majority, it is also known as "the capital of Latin America." This occurred with the continuing flight of Cubans from Communist Cuba starting in 1959 after the election of Fidel Castro. Before that its population was mostly comprised of refugees from the chilly Northeast. High on its list of tourist offerings is music, unique in the US due to the origins of its immigrants: Dominican *bachata* and *merengue*, Colombian *vallenato* and *cumbia*, Brazilian samba, and West Indian reggae, *soca, kompa, zouk*, calypso, and steel pan. Yum. There is a Winter Music Conference, and the Ultra Music Festival, too. They'll speak Spanish to you here.

For more traditional tourists, there are museums such as the Frost Art Museum, History Miami, Miami Art Museum, Miami Children's Museum, Miami Science Museum, Vizcaya Museum and Gardens, and the Miami-Dade Cultural Center. Tourist-oriented events and destinations include the Art Deco District in South Beach, Sony Ericsson Open, Art Basel, Winter Music Conference, South Beach Wine & Food Festival, and Mercedes-Benz Fashion Week Miami. The Everglades are only a short drive away, and Seminole (Miccosukee) Indians inhabit the area. In many ways this was America's last frontier, Miami having only 300 people in 1896. There is a subway, with bus and Amtrak connections. The cheapest flights to Latin American usually leave MIA.

Hostel Miami Beach, 236-9th St, Miami Beach, FL; *info@ hostelmiamibeach. com/*, T:+1(305)534.0268; $35Bed, Kitchen:Y, B'fast:Y, WiFi:Y, Pvt.room:Y, Locker:Y, Recep:24/7; Note: free meals, pool, billiards, bikes, luggage room, tour desk, parties

The South Beach Hostel, 235 Washington Ave, Miami Beach, FL; *southbeachhostel.com/*, T:+1(305)534.6669, *info@sobeho.com*; $19Bed, Kitchen:Y, B'fast:Y, WiFi:Y, Pvt.room:Y, Locker:Y, Recep:24/7; Note: arpt trans, resto/ bar, bikes, minimart, Espanol, parties, luggage room

Deco Walk Hostel, 928 Ocean Dr, Miami Beach, FL; *decowalkhostel.com/*, T:+1(305)531.5511, *decowalkhostel@gmail.com*; $30Bed, Kitchen:Y, B'fast:Y, WiFi:Y, Pvt.room:Y, Locker:Y, Recep:24/7; Note: bar, wheelchair OK, lift, luggage room, tour desk, parking, c.c. OK

Bikini Hostel, 1247 West Ave, Miami Beach, FL; *info@ bikinihostel. com/*, T:+1(305)253.9000; $20Bed, Kitchen:Y, B'fast:Y, WiFi:Y, Pvt.room:N, Locker:Y, Recep:24/7; Note: pool, billiards, tour desk, parking, laundry, luggage room

Jazz on South Beach Hostel, 321 Collins Ave, Miami Beach, FL; *southbeach@ jazzhostels.com/*, T:+1(305)672.2137; $45Bed, Kitchen:Y, B'fast:Y, WiFi:Y, Pvt.room:Y, Locker:Y, Recep: 24/7; Note: tour desk, ATM, laundry, luggage room, pancakes!

Tropics Hotel, 1550 Collins Ave, Miami Beach, FL; *email@ tropicshotel. com/*, T:+1(305)531.0361; $16Bed, Kitchen:Y, B'fast:N, WiFi:Y, Pvt.room:Y, Locker:N, Recep: 24/7; Note: arpt trans, pool, lift, wh/chair OK

Miami AAE World Hotel, 6300 Collins Ave, Miami Beach, FL; *miami. aaeworldhotels.com/*, T:+1(304)268.8981; $18Bed, Kitchen:Y, B'fast:N, WiFi:Y, Pvt.room:Y, Locker:Y, Recep:24/7; Note: resto/café, tour desk, parking

Freehand Miami, 2727 Indian Creek Dr, Miami FL; *Info.miami@ thefreehand. com/*, T:+1(305)531.2727; $25Bed, Kitchen:N, B'fast:Y, WiFi:Y, Pvt.room:Y, Locker:Y, Recep:24/7; Note: resto/bar, pool, bikes, tour desk, luggage room, party

Posh South Beach, 808 Collins Ave, Miami, FL; *poshsouthbeach.com/*, T:+1(561)398.7000, TF:877.762.3477; $27Bed, Pvt.room:N, Kitchen:Y, B'fast:Y, WiFi:Y, Locker:Y, Recep:24/7; Note: free arpt pickup, pool, lift, bar, tour desk, c.c. OK, modern

Miami Hostel, 810 Alton Rd, Miami, FL; *miamihostel.net/*, T:+1(305)538.7030;

$20Bed, Pvt.room:N, Kitchen:Y, B'fast:Y, WiFi:Y, Locker:Y, Recep:24/7; Note: party, free drinks, hot tub, billiards, wh/chair OK, nightclub

Santa Barbara Hostel, 230-20th St, Miami Beach, FL; T:+1(305)538.4411, *miami-santa-barbara.hostel.com/*; $17Bed, Pvt.room:Y, Kitchen:Y, B'fast:Y, WiFi:Y, Locker:Y, Recep:24/7; Note: old town, luggage room, tour info, basic

ORLANDO is a city of a quarter million located in south central Florida, with ten times that population in the metro area, and one of the country's fastest-growing. It receives more than fifty million tourists a year, mostly due to its plethora of theme parks, including Disney World, Universal Studios and others. It's a boy's dream.

Palm Lakefront Resort/Hostel, 4840 W Irlo Bronson Mem. Hwy, Kissimmee; *orlandohostels.com/*, T:+1(407)396.1759, *palmlakefront@yahoo.com*; $15Bed, Pvt.room:Y, Kitchen:Y, B'fast:N, WiFi:Y, Locker:Y, Recep:24/7; Note: gym, pool, bikes, shuttle, parking, tour desk, luggage room, laundry

World United Intl Hostel, 4640 W. Irlo Bronson Mem. Hwy (192), Kissimmee

World United Intl House, 4400 Simmons Rd., Orlando, FL; *orlando@worldunited.us/*, T:+1(347)600.9144; $25Bed, Pvt.room:Y, Kitchen:Y, B'fast:N, WiFi:Y, Locker:Y, Recep:ltd; Note: bar, pool, bikes, meals, parking, tour desk, arpt trans, laundry

TAMPA is the other big city in Florida, after Miami, with a Tampa Bay area total population of almost three million. It is famous for the Cuban cigars made in Ybor City, center of the Latino community. The mid-winter mock-invasion Gasparilla Pirate Festival is a hoot; so is Guavaween. There are Indian and LGBT film festivals.

Gram's Place BnB/Hostel, 3109 N Ola Ave, Tampa, FL; *grams-inn-tampa.com/*, T:+1(813)221.0596; $25Bed, Pvt.room:Y, Kitchen:Y, B'fast:N, WiFi:Y, Locker:Y, Recep:ltd; Note: music/GParsons theme, laundry, pub, nude swimming

7) Georgia

ATLANTA is Georgia's capital and largest city, with a metro-area population over five million. It has always been a major crossroads of the eastern seaboard and the Deep South, and today is a major world hub to boot, easily one of America's ten most important cities. Underground Atlanta is a good place to hang out and shop.

Atlanta Intl Hostel, 223 Ponce De Leon Ave NE, Atlanta, GA; T:+1(404)875.9449, *atlantainternationalhostel.com/*; $27Bed, Kitchen:Y, B'fast:Y, WiFi:Y, Pvt.room:N, Locker:Y, Recep:8a/11p; Note: nr Georgia Tech, 3-day cancel, upstairs balcony, trad house, nr mkt

Enota Mountain Retreat, 1000 Hwy 180, Hiawassee, GA; T:+1(706)896.9966, *enota.com/*, TF:800.990.8869; $21Bed, Pvt.room:Y, Kitchen:Y, B'fast:Y, WiFi:Y, Locker:N, Recep:24/7; Note: eco-retreat, resto, billiards, parking, luggage room, tour desk, safe dep

8) Hawaii

HAWAI'I (BIG ISLAND) is the largest of the Hawaiian Islands, with more than 4000sq.mi/10,000sq.km, including five volcanoes, some of them still active. The Great Crack is just the opposite, a deep fissure. Then there's the Hilna Slump, a chunk of Kilauea Volcano that is slumping away. King Kamehameha was from here, and eco-tourism is big, though agriculture is still important. Population is 185,000. Hilo is the main city, with over 43,000 people, a downtown area, and market.

Kirpal Meditation & Ecological Center, 13-260 Pohoiki Rd, Pahoa, HI; T:+1(808)333.9827, *admin@ kmechawaii.org/*; $30Bed, Kitchen:Y, B'fast:N, WiFi:Y, Pvt.room:Y, Locker:N, Recep:24/7; Note: tea/coffee, c.c. ok, parking

Cinderland Eco Village, 999 Four Corners, Pahoa, Hawaii, USA; *cinderlandecovillage.com/*, T:+1(808)936.5875, *cinderland1@gmail.com*; $10Bed, Kitchen:Y, B'fast:N, WiFi:N, Pvt.room:N, Locker:Y, Recep:ltd; Note: weekly rates, yoga, organic farm, cash only, arpt trans, bus, laundry

South Point Hostel, 93-2173 South Point Rd, Naalehu, HI, US; *southpointhostel. com/*, T:+1(808)929.7443, *mbassan@earthlink.net*; $23Bed, Kitchen:Y, B'fast:Y, WiFi:N, Pvt.room:N, Locker:N, Recep:ltd; Note: parking, luggage $, laundry, working farm

Hilo Backpackers Hostel, 69 Waianuenue Ave, Hilo, HI, US; *info@ hilobackpackershostel.com/*, T:+1(808)934.0800; $27Bed, Kitchen:N, B'fast:Y, WiFi:Y, Pvt.room:Y, Locker:N, Recep:ltd; Note: beer & pizza, arpt. pickup, near bus, tours

Hilo Bay Hostel, 101 Waianuenue Ave, Hilo Hawaii US; T:+1(808)933.2771, *sales@ hawaiihostel.net/*; $27Bed, Kitchen:Y, B'fast:N, WiFi:Y, Pvt.room:Y, Locker:Y, Recep:ltd; Note: tea/coffee, tour desk, parking, historic old bldg

Arnott's Lodge and Hiking Adventures, 98 Apapane Rd, Hilo, HI; T:+1(808)339.0921, *mahalo@ arnottslodge.com/*; $28Bed, Kitchen:N, B'fast:N, WiFi:Y, Pvt.room:Y, Locker:N, Recep:ltd; Note: parking, wheelchair ok, bikes, tour desk

Pineapple Park Volcano, 11-3489 Pikake St, Mt. View, TF:1(877)800.3800;

P'apple Pk Kona, 81-6363 Mamalahoa Hwy, Kealakekua T:+1(808)323.2224;

Hilo Airport Hostel, 860 Piilani St, Hilo, HI US; *pineapple-park.com/*; T:+1(808)430.5150, *park@aloha.net*; $28Bed, Kitchen:Y, B'fast:Y, WiFi:Y, Pvt.room:Y, Locker:Y, Recep:7a>9p; Note: arpt. pickup, parking, laundry, luggage room, billiards, bikes, pool

KOA Wood Hale/Patey's Place, 75-184 Ala Onaona St, Kailua-Kona, HI; T:+1(808)329.9663, *facebook.com/pages/Koa-Wood-Hale-Pateys-Place-Hostel*; $25Bed, Kitchen:Y, B'fast:N, WiFi:Y, Pvt.room:Y, Locker:Y, Recep:>10p; Note: parking, laundry, tour desk, bikes

KAUAI is the fourth-largest of the Hawaiian Islands, and has a population of over 65,000 people. Six million years old, it is geologically the oldest and one of the wettest places on earth, which has created some stunning erosion landscapes, including Waimea Canyon State Park, the "The Grand Canyon of the Pacific." Known also as the "Garden Isle", it's wild…and nice. Tourism is the main industry. A bus links the island. Kapaa is the largest town, with 10,000 inhabitants.

Kauai Beach House, 4-1546 Kuhio Hwy, Kapaa, HI; T:+1(808)823.8480, *kauaibeachhouse.net/*,; $35Bed, Kitchen:Y, B'fast:N, WiFi:Y, Pvt.room:Y, Locker:Y, Recep:ltd; Note: parking, laundry, luggage room, bikes, pool, ATM, a/c, c.c. ok

Honuea Intl Hostel Kauai, 4532 Lehua St, Kapaa, HI; T:+1(808)823.6142, *info@ honueahostel.com/*; $28Bed, Kitchen:Y, B'fast:N, WiFi:Y, Pvt.room:Y, Locker:Y, Recep:ltd; Note: parking, luggage $, safe dep, c.c. ok

MAUI is the second-largest of the Hawaiian Islands and has a population of 144,444, not a bad poker hand. It has volcanoes, rainforest, and whales for the watching. Whaling was once a major industry. Now it's agriculture and tourism, which suffers from over-growth and poor control. Hana Highway, Haleakala National Park, and Lahaina are the main destinations. Surfing and wind-surfing are big, and cruise ships call, all of which bring in a few million tourists and a few billion dollars, not bad for a small rural island.

The Northshore Hostel, 2080 West Vineyard St, Wailuku, Maui, Hawaii; T:+1(808)986.8095, *info@ northshorehostel.com/*; $33Bed, Kitchen:Y, B'fast:N, WiFi:Y, Pvt.room:Y, Locker:N, Recep:ltd; Note: arpt. pickup, parking, laundry, luggage room, safe deposit, c.c. ok

Lahaina Bungalow, 440 Wainee St, *lahainabungalow.blogspot.com/*, T:+1(808)214.4459, *lahainabungalow@gmail.com*; $35Bed, Kitchen:Y, B'fast:N, WiFi:Y, Pvt.room:Y, Locker:N, Recep:ltd; Note: 4N min, parking, a/c, c.c. ok, homestay, pet pig

Lahaina's Last Resort, 252 Lahainaluna Rd, Lahaina, HI, US; *lahainaslastresort.com/*, *T:+1(808)661.6655*, *reservations@oldlahaina.com*; $39Bed, Kitchen:N, B'fast:N, WiFi:N, Pvt.room:N, Locker:N, Recep:>7p; Note: tour desk, parking, club/bar, a/c, c.c. ok, central

Banana Bungalow Maui Hostel, 310 North Market St, Wailuku, HI; T:+1(808)244.5090, TF:18008HOSTEL, *info@ mauihostel.com/*; $37Bed, Kitchen:Y, B'fast:Y, WiFi:Y, Pvt.room:Y, Locker:N, Recep:ltd; Note: parking, laundry, luggage room, bikes, pool, hot tub, safe deposit

Hostel City Maui, 197 North Market St, Wailuku, HI; T:+1(808)244.0141;

Moped City Maui, 1898 Main St, Wailuku, HI, US; *mopedcitymaui.com/*, T:+1(808)495.0064, TF:1(800)820.820, *mopedcitymaui@gmail.com*; $27Bed, Kitchen:Y, B'fast:N, WiFi:Y, Pvt.room:Y, Locker:Y, Recep:24/7; Note: arpt. pickup, parking, safe dep, luggage rm, billiards, bikes, resto

Happy Valley Hale Hostel, 332 North Market St, Wailuku, HI; *nonalanicottages.com/*, T:+1(808)870.9100, *hvhale@earthlink.net*; $42Bed, Kitchen:Y, B'fast:N, WiFi:N, Pvt.room:Y, Locker:N, Recep:>8p; Note: cash, late checkin 6-8p fee, tea/coffee, TV, parking

OAHU is the third-largest and most populous of the Hawaiian Islands, with almost a million people. Honolulu, on the southeast coast, dominates the island. Its main beach at Waikiki is a symbol of fun 'n sun tourism, and if US mainlanders go to Maui, everybody else comes here. Besides the beach, there are the Bishop Museum, the Honolulu Zoo, the Waikiki Aquarium, Foster Botanical Garden, Lili'uokalani Botanical Garden, and Walker Estate, for starters. Then there are the Honolulu Museum of Art, The Contemporary Museum, the Hawaii State Art Museum, and the Hawaii International Film Festival.

Ho'o Nanea Hale, 59-222 Kamehameha Hwy, Haleiwa, HI; T:+1(808)781.6415, *info@ kalanihawaii.com/*; $47Bed, Kitchen:Y, B'fast:N, WiFi:Y, Pvt.room:Y, Locker:Y, Recep:ltd; Note: parking, laundry, luggage room, a/c, 3 night min, safe deposit, TV

Backpackers-Haleiwa, 59-788 Kamehameha Hwy, Haleiwa, HI; T:+1(808)638.7838, *info@ backpackers-hawaii.com/*; $31Bed, Kitchen:Y, B'fast:N, WiFi:Y, Pvt.room:Y, Locker:N, Recep:ltd; Note: parking, laundry, bikes, pool

Waikiki Backpackers Hostel, 2569 Cartwright Rd, Honolulu, HI: TF:1(866)404.4775, *info@ hostelsinhawaii.com/*; $29Bed, Kitchen:N, B'fast:Y, WiFi:Y, Pvt.room:Y, Locker:N, Recep:ltd; Note: Waikiki, arpt trans, pizza/beer, parking, laundry, luggage rm, bikes

Polynesian Hostel Beach Club, 2584 Lemon Rd #100, Honolulu, HI; *polynesianhostel.com/*, T:+1(808)922.1340, *polynesianhostel@gmail.com*; $23Bed, Kitchen:Y, B'fast:Y, WiFi:Y, Pvt.room:Y, Locker:Y, Recep:24/7; Note: tour desk, parking, laundry, luggage room, safe deposit, c.c. ok

HI Honolulu, 2323A Seaview Ave; T:+1(808)946.0591, *hihostel@lava.net*;

Hostelling International Waikiki, 2417 Prince Edward St, Honolulu, HI, US; *hostelsaloha.com/*, T:+1(808)926.8313, *waikiki@hiusa.org*; $25Bed, Kitchen:Y, B'fast:N, WiFi:Y, Pvt.room:N, Locker:Y, Recep:7a>3p; Note: no-party, long-stays, tour desk, parking, laundry, luggage $, c.c. ok

Waikiki Beachside Hostel 2556 Lemon Rd, Honolulu, HI; *waikikibeachsidehostel.com/*, T:+1(808)923.9566; $28Bed, Kitchen:Y, B'fast:Y, WiFi:Y, Pvt.room:N, Locker:Y, Recep:24/7; Note: luggage/towel fee, parking, laundry, a/c, c.c. ok, near beach

Stay Waikiki, 2424 Koa Ave, Honolulu, HI, US; T:+1(808)923.7829, *res@ stayhotelwaikiki.com/*; $35Bed, Kitchen:N, B'fast:Y, WiFi:Y, Pvt.room:Y, Locker:N, Recep:24/7; Note: "boutique", $10 amenity fee, tour desk, parking, laundry, a/c, c.c. ok

The Plumeria, 1111 Pikoi St, Honolulu, *plumeria.hostelalternative. com/*; T:+1(808)596.2080, *plumeria@hostelalternative.com*; $21Bed, Kitchen:Y, B'fast:N, WiFi:Y, Pvt.room:N, Locker:N, Recep:ltd; Note: long-stay rates, near transport/markets

Seaside Hawaiian Hostel, 419 Seaside Ave, Honolulu, HI; T:+1(808)924.3303, *resinfo@ seasidehawaiianhostel.com/*; $23Bed, Kitchen:Y, B'fast:N, WiFi:Y, Pvt.room:Y, Locker:N, Recep:ltd; Note: activities, theme nights

9) Idaho

BOISE is the capital and largest city of Idaho with a population of over a half million in the metro area. Downtown is the cultural center, with art, music, and a vibrant nightlife. There is a Basque Block, dedicated to the region's Basque heritage, and the classic Egyptian Theatre. Eighth Street is a pedestrian zone.

Ida Hostel, 280 N 8th St # 103, Boise, ID; *idahostel.com/*, T:+1(208)286.6476;$20Bed, Pvt.room:N, Kitchen:Y, B'fast:N, WiFi:Y, Locker:Y, Recep:3p>11p Note: central, pre-book only, wh/chair OK, parking, luggage rm, laundry

NAMPA is a suburb of Boise and a city of 80,000 in its own right.

Hostel Boise, 17322 Can-Ada Rd, Nampa, ID; T:+1(208)467.6858, *mail@ hostelboise.com/* ; $21Bed, Pvt.room:Y, Kitchen:Y, B'fast:Y, WiFi:Y, Locker:Y,

Recep:24/7; Note: arpt trans, parking, coffee/tea, rural nr Boise, B&B-ish, need car

SALMON is a town of three thousand in east Idaho, situated along Lewis and Clark's historic trail and near the Continental Divide. Sacajawea was born near here.

Century 2 Campground & RV Park, 603 Riverfront Dr, Salmon, ID: *century2campground.com/*, T:+1(208)756.2063; *century2campground@gmail.com*; $17Bed, Pvt.room:Y, Kitchen:Y, B'fast:N, WiFi:Y, Locker:N, Recep:ltd; Note: lockout 9-5, curfew 11p, luggage room, parking, river, forest

10) Illinois

CHICAGO is America's third largest city — after New York and LA — with a population 'city proper' of almost three million and greater 'Chicagoland' of at least 9M. It sits on Lake Michigan in Illinois with extended populations in neighboring states. O'Hare is now the second-busiest airport in the world, and it's always been that way, Chicago coming to prominence after its founding in 1833 as a transportation hub, especially railroads, linking east coast, Midwest, Great lakes, and great river, with the wide open spaces to the west. The Great Fire of 1871 almost burned it all down, but the World's Columbian Exposition in 1893 put it back in the world spotlight. In the early decades of the 20th century there was a mass migration of blacks to Chicago. There were also gangland killings connected to the imposition of alcohol prohibition. The 1960's saw Daley machine politics and the Democratic National Convention fiasco of 1968.

It's better now, all politics aside. Tourist attractions include the Adler Planetarium & Astronomy Museum, the Field Museum of Natural History, the Shedd Aquarium, the Art Institute of Chicago, Buckingham Fountain, the University of Chicago Oriental Institute, the Chicago History Museum, the Du Sable Museum of African American History, the Museum of Contemporary Art, the Peggy Notebaert Nature Museum, the Polish Museum of America, the Museum of Broadcast Communications, the Pritzker Military Library, the Chicago Architecture Foundation, and the Museum of Science and Industry. That should keep you busy. Chicago was a cradle for blues, soul, and rock music. There are Lollapalooza, Pitchfork, and Grants Park Music Festivals and a Taste of Chicago Festival for foodies. There is a Magnificent Mile and State Street for shoppers and strollers. There is a 150ft/46mt tall Ferris wheel, and a strong literary tradition. I've only been to Chicago once, back in 1972 to protest the Vietnam War; time to go back.

Chicago Parthenon Hostel, 310 S. Halsted St, Chicago, IL; *Reservations@ chicagoparthenonhostel.com/,* T:+1(312)258.1399; $31Bed, Kitchen:Y, B'fast:Y, WiFi:Y, Pvt.room:Y, Locker:Y, Recep:24/7; Note: resto/bar, near Amtrak/bus, near subway, laundry, ATM, maps central

IHSP Chicago at Damen CTA, 1616 N Damen Ave, Chicago, IL; *Info@ ihspusa.com/,* T/F:+1(304)268.8981; $31Bed, Kitchen:Y, B'fast:Y, WiFi:Y, Pvt. room:Y, Locker:Y, Recep:24/7; Note: arpt trans, laundry, luggage rm, 24/hr roof, mini-mart, bikes, prkg

Chicago Getaway Hostel, 616 W Arlington Pl, Chicago, IL; T:+1(773)929.5380, *getawayhostel.com/*; $35Bed, Kitchen:Y, B'fast:Y, WiFi:Y, Pvt. room:Y, Locker:Y, Recep:24/7; Note: arpt trans, bikes, luggage OK, laundry, parking $, billiards, lift

H.I. Chicago, 24 E Congress Pkwy, Chicago, IL; T:+1(312)360.0300, *reserve@ hichicago.org/*; $30Bed, Kitchen:Y, B'fast:Y, WiFi:Y, Pvt.room:Y, Locker:Y, Recep:24/7; Note: café, downtown, wheelchair OK, luggage rm, laundry, billiards

Urban Holiday Lofts, 2014 W. Wabansia Ave, Chicago, IL; *urbanholidaylofts. com,* T:+1(312)532.6949, *info@urbanholidayusa.com;* $26Bed, Kitchen:Y, B'fast:Y, WiFi:Y, Pvt.room:Y, Locker:Y, Recep:24/7; Note: bikes, luggage rm, laundry, tour desk, c.c. OK, tea/cof, a/c, nr L train

11) Indiana

INDIANAPOLIS (Indy) is Indiana's capital and largest city, topping two million in the larger metropolitan area. With ample opportunities for entertainment and shopping, its livability ratings are high, and it is most famous for the Indianapolis 500 auto race.

Indy Hostel, 4903 Winthrop Ave, Indianapolis, IN; *stay@ indyhostel.us/*, T:+1(317)727.1696; $29Bed, Pvt.room:N, Kitchen:Y, B'fast:N, WiFi:Y, Locker:N, Recep:24/7; Note: arpt trans, bikes, parking, tour desk, c.c. OK

12) Kansas

MARQUETTE is a town of 643 in the Smoky Hills region of Kansas, pure Americana.

Marquette Hostel, 117 N Washington, Marquette KS; *hostelmarquetteks. com/*, T:1(785)546.2455; *artspace115@gmail.com*; $20Bed, Pvt.room:Y, Kitchen:Y, B'fast:N, WiFi:Y, Locker:N, Recep:4p>6p; Note: parking, minimart, meals, c.c. OK, central, original art, Victorian bldg

13) Louisiana

LAFAYETTE is a cool little city of about 120,000, maybe half a million in the total Acadiana area—Cajun country—of which Lafayette is the unofficial capital. I was last here in 2006 for the Festival Louisiane, the country's best world music fest, an annual event sharing some performers and one weekend with the larger Jazz & Heritage Fest in New Orleans.

Blue Moon Guesthouse, 215 E Convent St, Lafayette, LA; T:+1(337)234.2422, *info@ bluemoonpresents.com/*; $18Bed, Pvt.room:N, Kitchen:Y, B'fast:N, WiFi:Y, Locker:Y, Recep:24/7; Note: central, bar/club, wh/chair OK, tour desk, laundry, parking, zydeco

NEW ORLEANS is the largest city in Louisiana, with over a million people in the metro area, and the birthplace of jazz music. It has cultural heritage from both France and Spain, which pre-date its American history as part of the Louisiana Purchase in 1804, though it is the French admixture which has endured, thanks to the flood of Acadians in the 1760's and Haitians in the early 1800's. The historic architecture is mostly from the Spanish era. With many free blacks, New Orleans fared better than most slave states in the Civil War. Today that vibrant hybrid-African culture expresses itself in music and culture. Mardi Gras is legendary and the Jazz and Heritage Festival is unsurpassed for good music, both in springtime. Hurricanes take a heavy toll, especially Katrina in 2005, from which the city has yet to fully recover. Besides jazz music, zydeco, Cajun, and rock are unique and popular. We Mississippians love to sin here, latest time for me in 2007.

India House Hostel, 124 S Lopez St, New Orleans, LA; *info@ indiahousehostel.com*, T:+1(504)821.1904; $17Bed, Pvt.room:Y, Kitchen:Y, B'fast:$, WiFi:Y, Locker:Y, Recep:24/7; Note: central, pool, bikes, tour desk, TV, terrace, meals $, parties

AAE Bourbon House Hostel, 1660 Annunciation St, New Orleans, LA; *bourbon.aaeworldhotels.com/*, T:+1(304)268.8981; *mraae@yahoo.com*; $26Bed, Pvt.room:Y, Kitchen:Y, B'fast:Y, WiFi:Y, Locker:Y, Recep:ltd; Note: bikes, minimart, tour desk, billiards, parking, forex, luggage room

St. Vincent's Guest House, 1507 Magazine St, New Orleans, LA; *stvguesthouse.com/*, T:+1(504)302.9606; *stvreservations@gmail.com*; $18Bed, Pvt. room:Y, Kitchen:Y, B'fast:$, WiFi:Y, Locker:N, Recep:ltd; Note: resto, parking, pool

14) Maryland

BALTIMORE is the largest city in the state and home to around 600K, down from its million-or-so 1950's peak, though still part of the huge multi-million conurbation that includes Washington, DC. Its status as a major port and manufacturing city has declined. I was here in 2004 to connect from BWI to NYC by bus at 2 a.m. It seemed OK, cheaper than DC I bet.

HI Baltimore, 17 W Mulberry St, Baltimore, MD; *baltimore@ hiusa.org/*, T:+1(410)576.8880; $22Bed, Pvt.room:N, Kitchen:Y, B'fast:Y, WiFi:Y, Locker:Y, Recep:24/7; Note: shuttle, parking, luggage rm, laundry, maps, common rm, trad house

KNOXVILLE is on the Potomac River, near the Harper's Ferry National Park.

HI Harper's Ferry Hostel, 19123 Sandyhook Rd, Knoxville, MD; *HarpersFerry@ hiusa.org/*, T:+1(301)834.7652; $18Bed, Pvt.room:N, Kitchen:Y, B'fast:Y, WiFi:Y, Locker:Y, Recep:7a/10p; Note: parking, laundry, @ Appalachian Tr, seasonal, camping, $250/nt/house

15) Massachusetts

BOSTON, MA is one of America's oldest cities and home to almost five million in the metro area. Its history goes back to 1630 and was instrumental in the events leading up to and including the Revolutionary War. Today it is one of America's most politically liberal cities. Faneuil Hall lies at the center of its tourist attractions. Boston Common is one of many parks in the city. Christian Science is to Boston what Scientology is to LA, and its Center, along with the Prudential Center, the library and Hancock Tower, are major landmarks. I was last here for a trade show back around 1992. I remember water, lots of it. The rental car agency made me show my gas receipt, weird...

Friend Street Hostel, 234 Friend St, Boston, MA; *info@ friendstreethostel.com/*, T:+1(617)934.24513; $43Bed, Kitchen:Y, B'fast:Y, WiFi:Y, Pvt.room:N, Locker:Y, Recep:24/7; Note: central, laundry, luggage rm, coffee/tea, meals $, cozy, c.c. OK

HI-Boston, 19 Stuart St, Boston, MA; *bostonhostel.org/*, TF:+1(888)464.4872; $40Bed, Kitchen:Y, B'fast:Y, WiFi:Y, Pvt.room:Y, Locker:Y, Recep:24/7; Note: café, lift, wheelchair OK, laundry, luggage rm, games, a/c, nr metro

CAPE COD is the easternmost portion of the state of Massahusetts, one of the largest barrier islands in the world, and the place where English history in the now-USA began. Nowadays it serves much the same function for Boston and the northeast that the central California coast serves for San Francisco and the contiguous urban area — a convenient and sublime getaway. The plethora of hostels — classic-style — reflect that. The original inhabitants were Wampanoag.

HI-Truro, North Pamet Rd, Truro; T:+1(508)349.3889, *truro@hiusa.org*

HI-Nantucket, Surfside, Nantucket; T:+1(508)228.0433, *nantucket@hiusa.org*

HI Hyannis, 111 Ocean St, Hyannis; T:+1(508)775.7990, *hyannis@hiusa.org;*

HI Eastham, 75 Goody Hallet Dr, Eastham; T:2552785, *eastham@hiusa.org*

HI-Martha's Vineyard, Edgartown-W. Tisbury Rd 525 W. Tisbury, MA; *capecod.hiusa.org/*, T:+1(508)693.2665, *vineyard@hiusa.org*; $32Bed, Pvt.room:N,

Kitchen:Y, B'fast:Y, WiFi:Y, Locker:M, Recep:7a/10p; Note: Cape Cod, parking, luggage room, seasonal, midday lockout

16) Minnesota

MINNEAPOLIS is Minnesota's largest city, and when paired with its 'twin city' — the capital of St. Paul — tops three million easily. This metropolis straddles the banks of the Mississippi River in its upper reaches, and is known as the "City of Lakes." Originally settled by Scandinavians, it was once known for its flour and timber; now it is better known for arts and culture. It's on my short list.

Minneapolis Intl Hostel, 2400 Stevens Ave. S, Minneapolis, MN; T:+1(612)874.0407, *reservations@ minneapolishostel.com*; $26Bed, Pvt.room:Y, Kitchen:Y, B'fast:N, WiFi:Y, Locker:N, Recep:10a>10p; Note: parking, left luggage $, Victorian mansion, basic

17) Nevada

LAS VEGAS is the largest city in Nevada, with over a half million people in the city proper, and one of the fastest-growing in the nation. It is most famous for its gambling industry, of course, which has evolved recently into hotels/casinos doubling as massive geographical/historical theme parks, e.g. Excalibur, Luxor, Bellagio, etc. 'The Strip' is the setting for most of this activity, while the Fremont District downtown preserves the original gambling district, and is much more walkable. Casinos also attract top entertainers.

Sin City Hostel, 1208 S Las Vegas Bl, Las Vegas, NV; *party@ sincityhostel.com/*, T:+1(702)868.0222; $12Bed, Kitchen:Y, B'fast:Y, WiFi:Y, Pvt.room:Y, Locker:Y, Recep:24/7 Note: wheelchair OK, laundry, luggage rm, basic, tour desk, job info

Las Vegas Hostel, 1322 Fremont St, Las Vegas, NV; *booking@ lasvegashostel. net/*, T:+1(702)385.1150; $17Bed, Kitchen:Y, B'fast:Y, WiFi:Y, Pvt.room:Y, Locker:Y, Recep:24/7; Note: pool, resto, not central, laundry, luggage rm, parking, lift, bus p-u

Hostel Cat, 1236 S Las Vegas Bl, Las Vegas, NV; *manager@ hostelcat.com/*, T:+1(702)380.6902; $12Bed, Kitchen:Y, B'fast:Y, WiFi:Y, Pvt.room:12, Locker:Y, Recep:ltd; Note: arpt trans, weekly rates, laundry, luggage rm, parking, tour desk, c.c.

RENO is Nevada's other famous gambling city, after Las Vegas, and by any other measure, as different from it as LA is from San Francisco. Nevada may not have any other measure. Population is about a quarter million; mountains and lakes lie near.

Wildflower Village, 4395 W. 4th St, Reno, NV; *wildflowervillage@ wildflowervillage.com/*, T:+1(775)747.8848; $30Bed, Pvt.room:Y, Kitchen:Y, B'fast:Y, WiFi:Y, Locker:N, Recep:ltd; Note: art haven, resto/bar, bikes, parking, books, luggage room, laundry

18) New Hampshire

CONWAY is a town of over 10,000 people surrounded by such natural attractions as White Mountain National Forest, Cathedral Ledge and Echo Lake state park.

White Mountains Hostel, 36 Washington St, Conway, NH; *stay@ whitemountainshostel.com/*, T:+1(603)447.1001; $27Bed, Pvt.room:N, Kitchen:Y, B'fast:N, WiFi:Y, Locker:N, Recep:8a/10p; Note: wh/chir OK, bikes, parking, need car

RUMNEY is a town of around 1500. It is located on the edge of the White Mountain National Forest.

D Acres Organic Farm/Homestead, 218 Streeter Woods Rd, Rumney; *info@ dacres.org/,* T:+1(603)786.2366; $17Bed, Pvt.room:Y, Kitchen:Y, B'fast:$, WiFi:Y, Locker:N, Recep:ltd; Note: cash only, home-grown food, eco-farm, resto, parking, tour desk

19) New Mexico

ALBUQUERQUE is New Mexico's largest city, with over a half million folks, and sits pretty much in the center of the state, at the junction of Interstate highways I-40 and I-25. It has a large Hispanic population, and a lively music scene. The hip capital of Santa Fe is about an hour away. I was last here in 2007 for the Globalquerque! world music festival, one of the USA's best. The best Mexican food in the USA is in this area.

The Route 66 Hostel, 1012 Central Ave SW, Albuquerque, NM; *rt66hostel. com/,* T:+1(505)247.1813, *rt66hostel@yahoo.com;* $20Bed, Kitchen:Y, B'fast:Y, WiFi:Y, Pvt.room:N, Locker:N, Recep:ltd; Note: central, nr clubs, trad house, long-stays

20) New York

BUFFALO is the state's second-largest city and lies far to the west on the narrow spit of land that separates Lakes Ontario and Erie, and connects the US to Canada at its southernmost peninsula, its Florida, so to speak. Toronto is only an hour away, after the border. Dress warmly. I was here for a Grateful Dead show around 1987, sold $1500 worth of Guatemalan textiles off the hood of my car, not bad, even saw Dylan with them — priceless.

Hostel Buffalo Niagara, 667 Main St, Buffalo, NY; *stay@ hostelbuffalo. com/*, T:+(716)852.5222; $25Bed, Pvt.room:Y, Kitchen:Y, B'fast:N, WiFi:Y, Locker:Y, Recep:8a/10p; Note: central, wh/chair OK, lift, luggage room, billiards, pubs

CAPE VINCENT is a town of almost three thousand in north-western New York at the point where the St Laurence seaway meets Lake Ontario — and the US meets Canada. It is also gateway to the '1000 islands,' good place to pre-mix your ketchup and mayo. There is a French presence here that dates back to Samuel Champlain's visits of 1615.

HI–Tibbetts Pt Lighthouse Hostel, 33439 Country Rt 6, Cape Vincent; *hihostels.com/*, T:1 315 654 3450, *tibbetspoint@hiusa.org*; $25Bed, Pvt.room:Y, Kitchen:Y, B'fast:N, WiFi:Y, Locker:Y, Recep:7/10p; Note: laundry, @Lake Ontario/St. Lawrence R., seasonal, old lighthouse qtrs

NEW PALTZ is a pleasant town of 7000 between Albany and New York City. There is a branch of the state university.

New Paltz Hostel, 145 Main St, New Paltz, NY; *newpaltzhostel.com/*, T:+1(845)255.6676, *NewPaltzHostel@yahoo.com*; $30Bed, Pvt.room:N, Kitchen:Y, B'fast:N, WiFi:Y, Locker:N, Recep:4p>10p; Note: nr bus station, parking, tour desk, luggage room, c.c. OK, laundry

NEW YORK CITY is arguably the most important city in the world, though you may not want to say that too loudly in LA. I'd say it's the capital, what with the United Nations there, and all that jazz. Hard to believe the Dutch once bought it for 60 guilders ($1000 in today's dollars). I'd've paid 62. By 1730 almost half of New York households owned slaves. After American defeat at the Battle of Long Island it became a haven for Loyalist refugees — and runaway slaves — during the Revolutionary War. It tried to secede from New York state, and the Union, along with the South in 1861. The Draft Riots of 1863 killed 100 blacks and drove the rest out of the city. From those humble beginnings, New York flourished to surpass London as the world's most populous city in the early 1920's, hitting ten million ten years later, the world's first megacity. At the same time it became a haven for the African diaspora, creating the Harlem Renaissance of arts and culture in the process. Tammany Hall machine politics was also replaced by... democracy.

Now it's the granddad of megacities, and proof that they can work. It has more skyscrapers than any city besides Hong Kong, including the One World Trade Center, to be completed this month, I believe. Besides New York's state parks, the city has 28,000 acres of municipal parkland, including Central Park, 883 acres in the center of it all. It now consists of five boroughs, four of them cities of over a million people in their own right. It was the cradle of jazz, punk, salsa, and disco musical styles, the abstract expressionist school of painting, and American theatre. It receives fifty million tourists a year, with prime destinations, such as the Empire State Building; Statue of Liberty; Ellis Island; Broadway theater productions; Metropolitan Museum of Art; Rockefeller Center; Times Square; Chinatown; Fifth and Madison Avenues. Then there are prime events such as Macy's Thanksgiving Day Parade; the St. Patrick's Day parade; the Tribeca Film Festival; and free performances in Central Park at Summerstage. Food's good, too. It's pricey... the city, not the food, one of the world's most expensive.

Equity Point New York, 206 W 41st St, New York, NY; *infonewyork@ equity-point.com/*, T:+1(212)703.8600; $69Bed, Kitchen:N, B'fast:Y, WiFi:Y, Pvt. room:Y, Locker:N, Recep:24/7; Note: nr Times Square, bar, lift, wh/chair OK, tour desk, c.c. OK

New York Budget Inn, 200 E 34th St, New York, NY; *info@ newyorkbudgetinn. com/*, T:+1(212)689.6500; $50Bed, Kitchen:N, B'fast:N, WiFi:Y, Pvt.room:Y, Locker:Y, Recep:24/7; Note: Midtown, TV, a/c, luggage room, c.c. OK

HI-New York, 891 Amsterdam Ave, New York, NY; *hinewyork.org/*, T:+1(212)932.2300; $54Bed, Kitchen:Y, B'fast:N, WiFi:Y, Pvt.room:N, Locker:Y, Recep:24/7; Note: arpt trans, café, wh/chair OK, lift, laundry, luggage room, tour desk

Q4 Hotel, 29-09 Queens Plaza N, Long Island City, NY; T:+1(718)706.7700, *info@ q4hotel.com/*; $37Bed, Pvt.room:Y, Kitchen:Y, B'fast:N, WiFi:Y, Locker:Y, Recep:24/7; Note: billiards, tour desk, laundry, luggage room, c.c. OK, Queens, subway

Jazz in the Park, 36 W 106th St, New York, NY; *park@ jazzhostels.com/*, T:+1(212)932.1600; $48Bed, Pvt.room:Y, Kitchen:N, B'fast:N, WiFi:Y, Locker:Y, Recep:24/7; Note: Central Park, billiards, tour desk, c.c. OK, no locals allowed

Chelsea Intl Hostel, 251 W 20th St, New York, NY; *chelseahostel.com/*, T:+1(212)647.0010; $48Bed, Pvt.room:Y, Kitchen:Y, B'fast:Y, WiFi:Y, Locker:Y, Recep:24/7; Note: Chelsea, arpt trans, ATM, c.c. OK

New York Loft Hostel, 249 Varet St, Brooklyn, NY; *nylofthostel.com/*, T:+1(718)366.1351; $60Bed, Pvt.room:Y, Kitchen:Y, B'fast:Y, WiFi:Y, Locker:Y, Recep:24/7; Note: ATM, TV, lift, luggage room, Brooklyn, take the L train

Broadway Hotel, 230 W 101st, New York, NY; *broadwayhotelnyc.com/*, T:+1(212)865.7710; $48Bed, Pvt.room:Y, Kitchen:Y, B'fast:N, WiFi:Y, Locker:Y, Recep:24/7; Note: cash only, lift, tour desk, meals, minimart, Central Park

The Bowery House, 220 Bowery, New York, NY; *info@ theboweryhouse. com/*, T:+1(212)837.2373; $74Bed, Pvt.room:Y, Kitchen:N, B'fast:N, WiFi:Y, Locker:Y, Recep:24/7; Note: Bowery, bikes, 300-thread-count sheets, a/c, cozy

American Dream Hostel, 168 E 24th St #1, New York, NY; *americandreamhostel.com/*, T:+1(212)260.9779; *AmericanDream24@aol.com*; $59Bed, Pvt.room:Y, Kitchen:Y, B'fast:Y, WiFi:Y, Locker:Y, Recep:24/7; Note: parking, luggage room, laundry, tea/coffee, Flatiron district

Chelsea Star Hotel, 300 West 30th St, NY; *chelseastar.com/*, T:1(877)827NYNY, *reservations@starhotelny*, $45Bed, Pvt.room:Y, Kitchen:N, B'fast:N, WiFi:Y, Locker:Y, Recep:24/7; Note: café, bikes, wh/chair OK, Midtown, luggage room, laundry, tour desk

Twelve Towns YMCA, 570 Jamaica Ave, Brooklyn; *ymcanyc.org/*, T:+1(917)441.8800, *gvillaverde@ymcanyc.org*; $60Bed, Pvt.room:Y, Kitchen:N, B'fast:N, WiFi:N, Locker:N, Recep:24/7; Note: pool, Brooklyn, parking, basic, far

Westway Hostel, 72-05 Astoria Bl, New York City, NY; *westwayhostel.com/*, T:+1(718)440.9696, *lghotelreservations@gmail.com*; $24Bed, Pvt.room:Y, Kitchen:Y, B'fast:N, WiFi:Y, Locker:Y, Recep:24/7; Note: nr arpt/subway, parking, c.c. OK, TV

Times Square Dream Hostel, 572-9th Ave, 1st Fl, New York City, NY; *timessquaredreamhostel.com/,* $49Bed, *timessquaredreamhostel@gmail.com;* Pvt. room:Y, Kitchen:Y, B'fast:N, WiFi:Y, Locker:Y, Recep:24/7; Note: 3N min, cash only, no alcohol

Intl Student Center, 38 W. 88th St, New York City, NY; *nystudentcenter.org/,* T:+1(212)717.7706; $30Bed, Pvt.room:N, Kitchen:Y, B'fast:N, WiFi:N, Locker:N, Recep:8a>11p; Note: midday lockout, luggage room, brownstone, max 7N, c.c. OK

NIAGARA FALLS is a city of 55K, across the border from the Canadian town of the same name, derived from the world-famous waterfalls which they share. The town is also part of the greater Buffalo metropolitan area. The city is attempting to reverse its industrial decline by promoting increased tourism. The water is awesome, of course.

Wanderfalls Hostel, 601 Spruce Ave, Niagara Falls, NY; *wanderfallshostel. com/,* T:+1(716)804.6235, *wanderfallshostel@gmail.com;* $26Bed, Pvt.room:Y, Kitchen:Y, B'fast:Y, WiFi:Y, Locker:Y, Recep:4p>9p; Note: nr bus, arpt trns, parking, tour desk, luggage room, laundry, walk>falls

SYRACUSE is a city of 660K in its metro area, in and around central New York State. There is an annual state fair… and a university. There is a jazz festival, a Shakespeare festival, and regular art events at Red House.

HI- Syracuse, 535 Oak St, Syracuse, NY; *hihostels.com/,* T:+1(315)472.5788, *syracusehostel@yahoo.com;* $25Bed, Pvt.room:Y, Kitchen:Y, B'fast:N, WiFi:Y, Locker:Y, Recep:7a//10p; Note: parking, luggage room, laundry, c.c. OK, 9-5 lockout

21) North Carolina

ASHEVILLE is a city of almost 100,000 and the largest in western North Carolina. As such it is one of the gateways to the Smoky Mountains and one of the few places where you can hear old-time 'bluegrass music' at its origins. People are friendly. I was last here in 1980 after hiking the Appalachian Trail.

Bon Paul and Sharky's Hostel, 816 Haywood Rd, Asheville, NC; *bonpaulandsharkys.com/*, T:+1(828)350.9929, *bpshostel@gmail.com*; $25Bed, Pvt. room:Y, Kitchen:Y, B'fast:N, WiFi:Y, Locker:Y, Recep:10a/10p; Note: parking, luggage room, tour desk, homey, central, res area, hot tub

BRYSON CITY is a way-station along the Appalachian Trail, in case sleeping in rat-infested bear-free shelters are not your cuppa'.

Aquone Hostel, 63 Britannia Dr, Nantahala, Topton, Bryson City, NC; *aquonelogcabinrentals.com/*, T:+1(828)321.2340, *margaretbennett@ peoplepc.com*; $20Bed, Pvt.room:Y, Kitchen:Y, B'fast:N, WiFi:Y, Locker:N, Recep:10a>8p; Note: shuttle to App. Trail, luggage rm, laundry, parking, hot tub, Smoky Mt.

22) Ohio

COLUMBUS is the Ohio state capital and largest city, with a million and a half people, half of them in the city proper. It is the home of Ohio State University, and has some notable bridges. It rates highly for biking and walking.

Wayfaring Buckeye Hostel, 2407 Indiana Ave, Columbus, OH; *mat@ wayfaringbuckeye.com/*, T:+1(614)754.0945; $23Bed, Pvt.room:Y, Kitchen:Y, B'fast:Y, WiFi:Y, Locker:Y, Recep:ltd; Note: bikes, parking, luggage rm, laundry, c.c. OK

Bessemer Hostel, 4592 Bessemer Rd, Nelsonville, OH; *bessemerhostel.com/*, T:+1(740)753.3000, *ckister@chadkister.com*; $10Bed, Pvt.room:Y, Kitchen:Y, B'fast:N, WiFi:Y, Locker:N, Recep:ltd; Note: billiards, parking, luggage rm, laundry, tour desk, forest

23) Oregon

ASHLAND is a small city of some 20,000, in southern Oregon along the I-5 corridor that leads to Portland to the north and the Siskiyou Mountains and California to the south. I was last here in 2002 to hear Ali Farka play in Lithia Park; killer sh*t.

Ashland Hostel, 150 N Main St, Ashland, OR; *admin@ theashlandhostel. com/,* T:+1(541)482.9217; $28Bed, Pvt.room:Y, Kitchen:Y, B'fast:Y, WiFi:Y, Locker:N, Recep:5p>8p; Note: trad house, parking, central, common room

EUGENE is a city of a few hundred thousand—Oregon's second largest—and the home of the University of Oregon. It is also known as a major capital of American hipness and environmental anarchy/activism. Ken Kesey was unofficial mayor for many years and the annual Oregon Country Fair in nearby Veneta is a direct link to the Acid Trips of the '60's. I saw the Grateful Dead there in 1982.

Eugene Whiteaker Intl Hostels, 970 W 3rd Ave, Eugene, OR; *eugenehostels. com/,* T:+1(541)343.3335, *eugenewhiteakerhostel@hotmail.com;* $23Bed, Pvt. room:Y, Kitchen:Y, B'fast:Y, WiFi:Y, Locker:N, Recep:ltd; Note: historic dist, tents OK, laundry, parking, games

PORTLAND is the largest city in Oregon—"last bastion of the terminally hip"—with a population of around 600K, four times that in the metro area. It sits on the Willamette River, near the Columbia. Parks and greenspaces are many, varied and important. This is Ecotopia; it rains like a mother. The Rose festival is held each June. The city rocks; microbreweries rule. I lived here 1981-84. Thank you, God. For more information, see the TV show 'Portlandia.'

HI – NW Portland Hostel, 425 NW 18th Ave, Portland, OR; *info@ nwportlandhostel.com/,* T:+1(503)241.2783; $22Bed, Pvt.room:N, Kitchen:Y, B'fast:Y, WiFi:Y, Locker:Y, Recep:24/7; Note: hip NW area, bikes, parking, wh/chair, luggage room, tour desk

AAE Portland Downtown, 415 SW Montgomery St, Portland, OR; *portlandor.aaeworldhotels.com/*, T:+1(304)268.8981; $28Bed, Pvt.room:Y, Kitchen:Y, B'fast:N, WiFi:Y, Locker:N, Recep:24/7; Note: downtown, nr Amtrak/bus, tour desk, parking, hotel/hostel

HI Portland, 3031 SE Hawthorne Bl, Portland, OR; T:+1(503)236.3380, *hip@ portlandhostel.org/*; $27Bed, Pvt.room:N, Kitchen:Y, B'fast:$, WiFi:Y, Locker:Y, Recep:ltd; Note: bikes, tour desk, parking, terrace, SE dist

Portland Pensione, 109 NE San Rafael St, Portland, OR; *portlandpensione. com/*, T:+1(503)288.4489, *portlandpensione@gmail.com*; $25Bed, Pvt.room:Y, Kitchen:Y, B'fast:N, WiFi:Y, Locker:N, Recep:24/7; Note: basic, NE nr Coliseum

24) Pennsylvania

PHILADELPHIA ('Philly') is second in size only to New York City on the US East Coast, with over four million in the metro area, almost half that in the city proper. It occupies a place in American history equaled or surpassed only perhaps by Boston, for it was here that the Declaration of Independence was signed and the constitutional convention was held. Those venues comprise most of the modern-day tourist attractions — Independence National Historical Park, and especially Independence Hall and the Liberty Bell.

Apple Hostels Philadelphia, 32 S Bank St, Philadelphia, PA; *philly@ applehostels.com/*, T:+1(215)922.0222; $34Bed, Pvt.room:N, Kitchen:Y, B'fast:N, WiFi:Y, Locker:Y, Recep:24/7; Note: downtown, luggage rm, laundry, tour desk, c.c.

HI - Chamounix Mansion, 3250 Chamounix Dr, Philadelphia, PA; *chamounix@ philahostel.org/*, T:+1(215)878.3676; $23Bed, Pvt.room:N,

Kitchen:N, B'fast:N, WiFi:Y, Locker:Y, Recep:8a/2a; Note: wh/chair OK, luggage room, parking, a/c, c.c. OK, trad mansion, far

25) Rhode Island

NEWPORT is a summer resort convenient to Providence and Boston, and home to the Naval War College. It has many colonial homes, and the center is a historic district. In addition to the famous folk festival, there is also a jazz festival and a film festival.

Newport Intl Hostel, 16 Howard St, Newport RI; *info@ newporthostel.com/*, T:+(401)369.0243; $20Bed, Pvt.room:N, Kitchen:Y, B'fast:N, WiFi:Y, Locker:Y, Recep:24/7; Note: seasonal, bikes, parking, tour desk, luggage room, maps

26) South Carolina

CHARLESTON, SC is a little gem of a small southern city. It is located on the Atlantic seaboard and has a history going back to 1670, well-preserved in its architecture, the main tourist attraction. It is also known for its friendliness and good manners. I was here once in the 80's to visit the nearby Gullah (Geechee) people, Afrricans who have preserved their culture and pidgin language to the present.

Not So Hostel, 156 Spring St, Charleston, SC; T:+1(843)722.8383, *info@ notsohostel.com/*; $26Bed, Kitchen:Y, B'fast:Y, WiFi:Y, Pvt.room:N, Locker:N, Recep:5p>10p; Note: advise late arrival, bikes, parking, 15 min>ctr, trad house

27) Tennessee

NASHVILLE is the second-largest city of Tennessee, capital of the state, and capital of American country music. If that's not enough, there is a full-scale reproduction of the Greek Parthenon. It's a democratic stronghold in a Republican state. It's also the northern terminus of the Natchez Trace Parkway. I haven't been here since the late 70's.

Music City Hostel, 1809 Patterson St, Nashville, TN; *info@ MusicCityHostel. com/*, T:+1(615)692.1277; $28Bed, Pvt.room:Y, Kitchen:Y, B'fast:N, WiFi:Y, Locker:Y, Recep:7a/10p; Note: arpt trans, bikes, parking, laundry, luggage rm

Nashville Downtown Hostel, 177 First Ave. North, Nashville, TN; *info@ nashvillehostel.com/*, T:+1(615)497.1208; $26Bed, Pvt.room:N, Kitchen:Y, B'fast:N, WiFi:Y, Locker:Y, Recep:24/7; Note: shuttle, bar, wh/chair OK, laundry, luggage room, lift, games, books

28) Texas

AUSTIN is Texas's state capital and home to over half a million, an oasis of progressive politics in an otherwise conservative South. It is also one of the coolest places in the US and the world. The music scene is legendary, and the haunt of many an alt-country folk-rocker. During SXSW the whole of downtown becomes one huge music and film showcase, including indie, rock and world music. The ACL festival ain't bad, either. Tell Willie I said hey. To the east is the wooded south; to the west are dry plains. Lakes are nice.

HI Austin, 2200 S Lakeshore Blvd, Austin, TX; *hiusa.org/Austin/*, T:+1(512)444.2294; $22Bed, Kitchen:Y, B'fast:Y, WiFi:Y, Pvt.room:Y, Locker:Y,

Recep:24/7; Note: no alc, Town Lake, parking, wheelchair OK, SXSW/ACL surcharge

Firehouse Hostel, 605 Brazos St, Austin, TX; *firehousehostel.com/*, T:+1(512)201.2522; *austinfirehouse@gmail.com;* $29Bed, Pvt.room:Y, Kitchen:Y, B'fast:Y, WiFi:Y, Locker:Y, Recep:24/7; Note: bar/club, wh/chair OK, lift, luggage room, laundry

EL PASO is a city of over 600,000 in far west Texas, due south of Albuquerque, New Mexico. It sits on the Rio Grande (*Rio Bravo del Norte*) across the border from Ciudad Juarez in Mexico. My first foray into a 3rd World country occurred right here back in 1974. It was pretty wild then. I hear it still is… in a different way. I haven't been back.

Gardner Hotel-El Paso Hostel, 311 E Franklin Ave, El Paso, TX; *info@ gardnerhotel.com/*, T:+1(915)532.3661; $27Bed, Pvt.room:Y, Kitchen:Y, B'fast:N, WiFi:Y, Locker:Y, Recep:24/7; Note: downtown, laundry, billiards, antique hotel, lift, a/c, Mexico border

HOUSTON is Texas's largest city and fourth largest in the nation. It is famous for its NASA Johnson Space Center and Mission Control Center. It is a major gulf port and center of the petroleum industry. The Theater and Museum districts head up the cultural offerings on hand. The beach at nearby Galveston is a nice day trip. The weather is warm and humid. This is the south.

HI Houston, 501 Lovett Blvd, Houston, TX; *hiusa.org/Houston/*, T:+1(713)636.9776; $23Bed, Kitchen:Y, B'fast:Y, WiFi:Y, Pvt.room:N, Locker:Y, Recep:24/7; Note: pool, parking, terrace, laundry, luggage room, tea/coffee, trad house

Houston Intl Hostel, 5302 Crawford St, Houston, TX; *resv@ houstonhostel. com/*, T:+1(713)523.1009; $17Bed, Kitchen:Y, B'fast:N, WiFi:$, Pvt.room:Y, Locker:N, Recep:ltd; Note: central museum district, luggage room, laundry, parking, pub trans

29) Utah

PARK CITY is a town of 7-8000 that sits up in the mountains 20mi/32km southeast of Salt Lake City. Once a mining town, it is now a major tourist destination, mostly for its winter sports. It is also home to the world's largest independent film festival, Sundance. There are more tourists than residents.

AAE Chateau Lodge, 1299 Norfolk Ave, Park City, UT; *chateauapres. com/*, T:+1(435)6499372, *chateauapres@gmail.com*; $40Bed, Pvt.room:N, Kitchen:N, B'fast:Y, WiFi:Y, Locker:Y, Recep:ltd; Note: parking, ski resort

SALT LAKE CITY is the capital and largest city of Utah, with a couple hundred thousand inhabitants, and five times that in the metro area. It is perhaps best known as the home of the Church of Latter-Day Saints (Mormon). It is also a mountain city, with the Winter Olympics in 2002, Park City playing Aspen to its Denver only a short hour's drive away.

Avenues Hostel, 107 N. 'F' St, Salt Lake City, UT; *Info@ saltlakehostel. com/*, T:+1(801)539.8888; $17Bed, Pvt.room:Y, Kitchen:Y, B'fast:Y, WiFi:Y, Locker:Y, Recep:ltd; Note: hot tub, wh/chair OK, bikes, parking, luggage room, central

Camelot Inn & Hostel, 165 W 800 S, Salt Lake City, UT; *ut123.com/*, T:+1(801)688.6196, *artur4@hotmail.com*; $18Bed, Pvt.room:Y, Kitchen:Y, B'fast:N, WiFi:Y, Locker:Y, Recep:ltd; Note: wh/chair OK, bikes, parking, luggage rm, central, TV, self-checkin

Utah International Hostel, 50 S 800 W, Salt Lake City, UT; T:801.359.4525, *utahinternationalhostel.com/*; $20Bed, Pvt.room:Y, Kitchen:Y, B'fast:N, WiFi:Y, Locker:Y, Recep:9a>10p; Note: central, arpt trans, parking, laundry, basic

30) Vermont

BURLINGTON is the largest city in Vermont, albeit with a population barely exceeding 40,000, and five times that many in the metro area, or one-third of the state's total. It sits on Lake Champlain. Church Street Marketplace is a pedestrian mall, venue for festivals and good place to people-watch.

Burlington Hostel, 53 Main St, Burlington, VT; *info@ theburlingtonhostel. com /*, T:+1(802)540.3043; $35Bed, Pvt.room:N, Kitchen:Y, B'fast:Y, WiFi:Y, Locker:Y, Recep:3p>10p; Note: winter curfew 10p, luggage room, midday lockout, waffles!

31) Virginia

CHARLOTTESVILLE is a small city of some 45,000 best known as the birthplace of presidents Jefferson and Monroe. Nearby is the UNESCO world heritage site that includes Jefferson's Monticello home and the University of Virginia. There is a downtown pedestrian mall and several music venues. Shenandoah National Park is nearby with scenic Skyline Drive, an extension of the Blue Ridge parkway.

Alexander House, 1205 Monticello Rd, Charlottesville, VA; *booking@ alexanderhouse.us/*, T:+1(434)327.6447; $30Bed, Pvt.room:N, Kitchen:Y, B'fast:Y, WiFi:Y, Locker:$, Recep:2p>10p; Note: bikes, parking, cash only, near Univ/ dntn mall

32) Washington

BINGEN is a town of less than a thousand on the Columbia River gorge, known for its good windsurfing, among other things. Portland, OR, is only an hour away. The volcanic Mount St. Helens is nearby. Mount Hood and the Hood River are on the other side. The ex and I won the dance contest in nearby Trout Creek back in 1982.

The Bingen School Inn, Cedar/Humboldt Sts, Bingen, WA; *Info@ bingenschool.com/*, T:+1(509)493.3363; $19Bed, Pvt.room:Y, Kitchen:Y, B'fast:N, WiFi:N, Locker:Y, Recep:6a>9p; Note: nr Mt. St. Helens, resto, gym, parking, windsurfing, Natl Scenic Area

PORT ANGELES is a town of some 19,000 that sits on the north end of the Olympic peninsula. Through some stroke of luck Port Angeles apparently sits in the rain shadow of the Olympic Mountains, so gets much less rain than other areas, lucky it. This is where you get the ferry boat to Victoria, BC, Canada.

Toad Lily House, 105 E 5th St, Port Angeles, WA; *booking@ toadlilyhouse. com/*, T:+1(360)797.3797; $25Bed, Pvt.room:Y, Kitchen:Y, B'fast:N, WiFi:Y, Locker:Y, Recep:9a>5p; Note: wh/chair OK, meals, parking, tour desk, luggage room, laundry

SEATTLE is the largest city of Washington state and the Pacific Northwest region, with a metro area of over four million. It is also one of the coolest, figuratively, with a beauty to rival San Francisco on and around the banks of the Puget Sound. It is also part of the hip strip of alternative lifestyles and liberal politics stretching from Vancouver to the north and down south past Eugene and on to San Francisco. Boeing, Microsoft, and Starbucks all call it (corporate) home. Pike's Place Market is a great place to browse and hang out. Fremont district is a great place to stay. They also have a cool street fair. Bumbershoot is a bigger one over at Seattle Center downtown. That's where the Space Needle is, and ground zero for tourism here. I stayed on a houseboat here back in 1978. My last visit was in 2007.

City Hostel Seattle, 2327 2nd Ave, Seattle, WA; *reservations@ hostelseattle. com/*, T:+1(206)706.3255; $28Bed, Pvt.room:Y, Kitchen:Y, B'fast:Y, WiFi:Y, Locker:Y, Recep:9a>11p; Note: hot tub, luggage room, laundry, terrace

HotelHotel Hostel, 3515 Fremont Ave. N, Seattle; *hello@ hotelhotel.co/*, T:+1(206)257.4543; $26Bed, Pvt.room:Y, Kitchen:Y, B'fast:Y, WiFi:Y, Locker:N, Recep:>11p; Note: bikes, maps, hip Fremont

Green Tortoise, 105 Pike St, Seattle, WA; *greentortoise.net/*, T:+1(206)340.1222; $31Bed, Pvt.room:N, Kitchen:Y, B'fast:Y, WiFi:Y, Locker:Y, Recep:24/7; Note: bikes, forex, meals, tour desk, luggage room, laundry, Pike's Place

Second Home Hostels, 19201-33rd Ave S, SeaTac, WA; *secondhomehostels. com/*, T:+1(206)497.4517; $25Bed, Pvt.room:N, Kitchen:Y, B'fast:Y, WiFi:Y, Locker:Y, Recep:7a>11p; Note: wh/chair OK, tour desk, luggage room, laundry, parking, walk>arpt

HI at the American Hotel, 520 S. King St, Seattle, WA; *hiusa.org/seattle/*, T:+1(206)299.4141; $29Bed, Pvt.room:Y, Kitchen:Y, B'fast:Y, WiFi:Y, Locker:Y, Recep:24/7; Note: lift, wh/chair OK, tour desk, luggage room, laundry, Chinatown

33) Wisconsin

MADISON is a city of more than a half million in the metro area, with maybe half in the city proper, and capital of the state of Wisconsin. It is perhps better known as the home of the University of Wisconsin, whose students made it a capital of 60's counterculture and a bastion of liberalism today. That also makes it a pretty cool place to hang, with vast opportunities for music, festivals, and other forms of entertainment.

HI Madison Hostel, 141 S Butler St, Madison, WI; *madison@ hiusa.org/*, T:+1(608)441.0144; $22Bed, Pvt.room:Y, Kitchen:Y, B'fast:N, WiFi:Y, Locker:Y, Recep:8a>10p; Note: café, parking, luggage room, bikes

34) Wyoming

JACKSON HOLE is a valley in western Wyoming near the border with Idaho. The Teton Mountains and surrounding countryside are the big attraction.

The Hostel, 3315 Village Dr, Teton Village, WY; *info@ thehostel.us/*; T:+1(307)733.3415; $18Bed, Pvt.room:N, Kitchen:Y, B'fast:N, WiFi:Y, Locker:N, Recep:ltd; Note: parking, TV, billiards, luggage room, laundry, mountains, games

Part II: Canada

Canadians, bear with me here, please, but many Americans know little of our northern neighbor, the world's second-largest country and home to almost 35 million souls, bilingual and multi-cultural and strung along our northern border. The early history is much the same, of course, proto-Indians pushing south from the polar regions, the first among them leaving myriad unspecified progeny, later groups such as the Athabaskans leaving very specific progeny in northwestern Canada and as far south as Arizona and Mexico, and finally Eskimos (Inuit) following that same northern path and then pushing east instead of south in one of the largest migrations ever known, all the way to Greenland. When the Europeans finally came, it was the French first, with Jacques Cartier in 1534, but nothing much happened until the founding of Quebec by Champlain in 1608. The rest is history.

The English followed soon after with colonies on Newfoundland and further south. That's us. The French-and-Indian (Intercolonial) Wars attempted to delineate the limits of each country's influence, without much luck until recognition of American independence in 1783. The War of 1812 revisited the issues. After that immigration to Canada began to pick up stream. The Oregon Treaty of 1846 revisited the same issues — who gets what — again. This last treaty opened up Vancouver Island and British Columbia for immigration and soon there was nothing left but to fill in the empty space between. The Canada Confederation was created in 1867. The maple-leaf flag was adopted in 1965, and Canada finally cut the cord legally with Great Britain in 1982. Meanwhile French-speaking Quebec has been threatening secession for the last fifty years, but has yet to actually do it. Keep your fingers crossed.

Today Canada is one of my favorite places, something like the best of all possible worlds, except for the climate, a huge vast display of Nature, in addition to some really nice cities, without all the imperial baggage that the US has to carry around as part of its historical legacy. True, Canada is still more attached to the United Kingdom than seems necessary or desirable to me, but the results are splendid. Cities are more organic than those of the US, without all the hollow cores and ultra-suburban lifestyles that define so much of the US. If it weren't so cold, they'd really have something here.

Bring on the global warming (just kidding)! The hostel situation seems a little better, too, though not as much as I'd hoped. Still it has half as many as the US with only one-tenth the population, so that speaks volumes. Anybody care to open one in Yellowknife? It's on my list... Canada does have one thing that many—if not most—countries lack, and that's a centralized website/ database for hostels: *www.backpackers.ca*, helpful.

35) Alberta

BANFF NATIONAL PARK is located in the southern Alberta Rocky Mountains, along the border with British Columbia to the west and contiguous with Jasper National Park to the north. Banff town is located due west of Calgary via Canmore, and is something of a tourist zoo of 7500 residents, pubbing and clubbing and snubbing. Both the highway and railway go right through. The park is something else, mountains and lakes and streams and wildlife in random profusion, for an American probably most similar to Glacier National Park to the immediate south in Montana, God's country.

HI-Banff Alpine Centre, 801 Hidden Ridge Way, Banff, AB; *hihostels.ca/ westerncanada/*, T:+1(403)762.4123; $32Bed, Pvt.room:Y, Kitchen:Y, B'fast:Y, WiFi:Y, Locker:Y, Recep:24/7; Note: arpt trans, resto/bar, bikes, wh/chair OK, parking, luggage rm, laundry

Y Mountain Lodge, 102 Spray Ave, Banff, AB; *ymountainlodge.com/*, T:+1(403)762.3560; $36Bed, Pvt.room:Y, Kitchen:Y, B'fast:$, WiFi:$, Locker:N, Recep:24/7; Note: arpt trans, resto/bar, books, parking, luggage rm, laundry, lift, TV

HI-Rampart Creek, Hwy 93, Banff National Park, Alberta

HI-Hilda Creek, Hwy 93, Banff National Park, Alberta

HI-Castle Mountain, Hwy 1A & Hwy 93 S, Banff National Park, AB: *hihostels.ca/westerncanada/*, T:+1(778)328.2220; TF:+1(866)762.4122; $23Bed, Pvt.room:N, Kitchen:Y, B'fast:N, WiFi:N, Locker:N, Recep:>10p; Note: parking, wilderness, no power, no flush toilets, solar lights

Samesun Banff, 433 Banff Ave, Banff, AB; T:+1(403)762.4499, *samesun. com/*, TF:1.877.9.SAMESUN; $32Bed, Pvt.room:N, Kitchen:Y, B'fast:Y, WiFi:Y, Locker:Y, Recep:ltd; Note: billiards, luggage room, laundry, parking

Banff International Hostel, 449 Banff Ave, Banff, AB; T:+1(403)985.7744, *info@ banffinternationalhostel.com/*, TF:+1.855.5.HOSTEL; $32Bed, Pvt.room:Y, Kitchen:Y, B'fast:Y, WiFi:Y, Locker:Y, Recep:24/7; Note: forex, TV, ATM, billiards, luggage room, laundry, parking

CALGARY is the largest city in Alberta and the third to fifth largest in Canada, depending on how you count. It is famous for its Calgary Stampede rodeo every July. The Film Festival, Folk Music Festival, FunnyFest, Greek Festival, Carifest, Wordfest, Lilac Festival, GlobalFest, Fringe Festival, Summerstock, Expo Latino, Gay Pride, and Spoken Word Festival aren't bad, either. I was last here in 2011. It rocks. I like.

Wicked Hostel, 1505 Macleod Trail SE, Calgary, AB; *bookings@ wickedhostel. com/*, T:+1(403)265.8777; $30Bed, Pvt.room:N, Kitchen:Y, B'fast:Y, WiFi:Y, Locker:N, Recep:ltd; Note: bikes, parking, luggage rm, laundry, party, books, games, long-stays

HI-Calgary City Centre, 520 7 Ave SE, Calgary, AB; *hihostels.ca/ westerncanada/*, T:+1(778)328.2220; $30Bed, Pvt.room:N, Kitchen:Y, B'fast:Y, WiFi:Y, Locker:Y, Recep:24/7; Note: East Village, central, bikes, billiards, parking, luggage rm, laundry

CANMORE is the town between Banff and Calgary, right off the main highway, and something of a nice alternative to both of them, genuine small town and nature, too.

HI-Canmore, 201 Indian Flats Rd, Canmore, AB; T:+1(403)678.3200; *hihostels.ca/westerncanada/*, $25Bed, Pvt.room:N, Kitchen:Y, B'fast:N, WiFi:Y, Locker:Y, Recep:ltd; Note: arpt trans, parking, luggage room, laundry, tour desk

The Hostel Bear, 1002 Bow Valley Trail, Canmore, AB; T:+1(403)678.1000, *info@ thehostelbear.com/*; $34Bed, Pvt.room:Y, Kitchen:Y, B'fast:N, WiFi:Y, Locker:Y, Recep:24/7; Note: bar, wh/chair OK, parking, luggage rm, laundry, tour desk, billiards

EDMONTON is Alberta's other major city — besides Calgary — with a population over 800K in the city proper, over a million in the metro area. It is the staging ground for ventures into the Northwest Territories and the Tar Sands at Fort McMurray. It has the largest mall in North America, featuring its own beach, surf not usually a problem. Old Strathcona is the historic district, with plenty of entertainment, too. The Edmonton Folk Festival is one of the world's best. I came for it in 2007, featuring Andy Palacios, r.i.p. At fifty-four degrees north latitude, chances of seeing the northern lights are not bad.

HI Edmonton, 10647-81 Ave NW, Edmonton AB; *hihostels.ca/*, T:+1(780)988.6836; $27Bed, Pvt.room:Y, Kitchen:Y, B'fast:N, WiFi:Y, Locker:Y, Recep:24/7; Note: Old Strathcona, minimart, pool, billiards, parking, luggage rm, tours

GO Backpackers Hostel, 10209-100ᵗʰ Ave NW, Edmonton, AB; *edmonton@ gohostels.ca/*, T:+1(780)423.4146; $26Bed, Pvt.room:N, Kitchen:Y, B'fast:N, WiFi:Y, Locker:Y, Recep:24/7; Note: tour desk, luggage room, wh/chair OK, lift, billiards, laundry

JASPER NATIONAL PARK is the largest national park in the Canadian Rockies and a UNESCO world heritage site. Attractions include Mount Edith Cavell, Pyramid Lake and Pyramid Mountain, Maligne Lake, Medicine Lake, Tonquin Valley, Marmot Basin ski area, Athabasca Glacier, the Columbia Icefield, Athabasca Falls, Jasper Tramway, and the Miette Hot Springs. The Icefields Parkway — 140mi/230km in length — connects Lake Louise, Alberta, in Banff National Park, to Jasper, Alberta. The town of Jasper (pop. 4000+/-) services the park and visitors.

HI Jasper, 1 Skytram Rd, Jasper, AB; *hihostels.ca/westerncanada/*, T:+1(780)852.3215; $23Bed, Pvt.room:N, Kitchen:Y, B'fast:N, WiFi:Y, Locker:Y, Recep:ltd; Note: 7km>town/train, minimart, bikes, tour desk, luggage room, parking

HI-Mount Edith Cavell, Cavell Road, Jasper National Park, AB

HI-Beauty Creek, Highway 93, Jasper National Park, AB

HI-Maligne Canyon, Maligne Lake Rd, Jasper National Park, AB

HI-Athabasca Falls, Highway 93, Jasper National Park, AB; *hihostels.ca/ westerncanada/*, T:+1(778)328.2220; TF:+1(866)762.4122; $23Bed, Pvt.room:N, Kitchen:Y, B'fast:N, WiFi:N, Locker:N, Recep:>10p; Note: parking, wilderness, no power, no flush toilets, solar lights

KANANASKIS is system of parks located in the foothills and front ranges of the Rockies west of Calgary. It is a mixed-use area, with timber, oil, and cattle industries, in addition to tourism. The village hosted a G8 summit meeting in 2002, not too shabby.

HI-Kananaskis, 1 Ribbon Creek Road, Kananaskis, AB; *hihostels.ca/ westerncanada/*, T:+1(778)328.2220; TF:1(866)762.4122; $23Bed, Pvt.room:Y, Kitchen:Y, B'fast:N, WiFi:N, Locker:N, Recep:>10p; Note: parking, wilderness, midday lockout, closed Mondays (by season)

LAKE LOUISE is a village of about 1000 residents, named after and servicing the nearby lake of the same name. Lake's sublime, too, reflections like a Rorshach test from Nature. Listen to Gram Parsons sing "Blue Canadian Rockies;" he says it better than I.

HI Lake Louise, 203 Village Rd, Lake Louise, Alberta; T:+1(778)328.2220, *hihostels.ca/westerncanada/*, TF:1(866)762.4122; $25Bed, Pvt.room:Y, Kitchen:Y, B'fast:N, WiFi:Y, Locker:Y, Recep:ltd; Note: all-year, resto, luggage rm, laundry, tour desk, lift, sauna, wh/chair

NORDEGG is a village of a couple hundred in west-central Alberta, at an elevation of 4200ft/1300mt. It was originally founded as a coal-mining town, now a national historic site. There are many parks in the area.

HI Nordegg, Shunda Creek, Nordegg, AB; *hihostels.com/*, TF:1(888)748.6321, *shunda@hihostels.ca*; $28Bed, Pvt.room:N, Kitchen:Y, B'fast:N, WiFi:N, Locker:Y, Recep:9a/11p; Note: hot tub, bikes, parking, laundry, c.c. OK

36) British Columbia

BIG WHITE is a ski resort east of Vancouver in southern British Columbia, on Big White Mountain. Night skiing, anyone? Shopping?

The Urban Retreat Hostel, 7470 Porcupine Rd, Big White, BC; *urbanretreathostel.com/*, T:+1(250)765.7920, *bigwhitehostel@berezanhg.com*; $30Bed, Pvt.room:Y, Kitchen:Y, B'fast:N, WiFi:Y, Locker:Y, Recep:ltd; Note: luggage room, parking, midday lockout, c.c. OK

DENMAN ISLAND is one of the Gulf Islands off the coast of Vancouver Islands and linked to it by ferry. It has over 1000 full-time residents and is a center of alternative lifestyles.

Denman Island Guesthouse Hostel, 3806 Denman Rd, Denman Island, BC; *Sheldon@ info@ earthclubfactory.com/*, T:+1(250)335.2688; $24Bed, Pvt. room:N, Kitchen:N, B'fast:N, WiFi:Y, Locker:N, Recep:ltd; Note: resto, laundry, music, events, alternative lifestyles

FERNIE is a city of almost 5000 at an elevation of 3300ft/1000mt, and totally surrounded by Rocky Mountains. Once a center of coal mining, the emphasis is now on tourism, wise choice. This is historic architecture, and winter sports are good.

The Raging Elk Intl Hostel Fernie, 892 - 6 Ave, Fernie, BC; *bookings@ ragingelk.com/*, T:+1(250)423.6811; $26Bed, Pvt.room:N, Kitchen:Y, B'fast:Y, WiFi:Y, Locker:Y, Recep:24/7; Note: billiards, parking, luggage room, tour desk, bikes, pancakes!

GOLDEN is a town of almost 4000 nestled in a valley at 2600ft/800mt amidst surrounding ridges. Once dependent on logging and the railroad, it is now diversified into tourism and related services, such as paragliding, hang gliding, mountain biking… and stranded drivers.

Dreamcatcher Hostel Ltd, 528-9 Ave N, Golden, BC; T:+1(250)439.1090, *Info@ dreamcatcherhostel.com/*; $35Bed, Pvt.room:Y, Kitchen:Y, B'fast:N, WiFi:Y,

Locker:Y, Recep:ltd; Note: non-party, parking, luggage room, wh/chair OK, cafe, laundry

Kicking Horse Hostel, 518 Station Ave, Golden, BC; *kickinghorsehostel. com/*, T:+1(250)344.5071; $31Bed, Pvt.room:Y, Kitchen:Y, B'fast:N, WiFi:Y, Locker:Y, Recep:ltd; Note: parking, luggage room, games, books, walk everywhere

Caribou Hostel, 1401 Adolph Johnson Rd, Golden, BC; *info@ caribouhostel. ca/*, T:+1(250)344.4870; $31Bed, Pvt.room:Y, Kitchen:Y, B'fast:N, WiFi:Y, Locker:N, Recep:ltd; Note: cash only, out of town, resto, parking, luggage room, wh/chair OK

KELOWNA is a city on Okanagan Lake in Okanagan Valley, with a population of 100K or two, so a pretty large one, too. Its mythical lake monster is named Ogopogo, yep. There are festivals in the summer and skiing in the winter. There are vineyards, too.

Kelowna SameSun Backpacker Lodge, 245 Harvey Ave, Kelowna, BC; *samesun.com/*, TF:1(877)972.6378; $27Bed, Pvt.room:Y, Kitchen:Y, B'fast:Y, WiFi:Y, Locker:Y, Recep:ltd; Note: Okanagan Lake/valley, nightlife, luggage rm, laundry, tour desk

Kelowna Intl Hostel, 2343 Pandosy St, Kelowna, BC; *kelowna-hostel.bc.ca/*, T:+1(250)763.6024, *kelownahostel@silk.net*; $21Bed, Pvt.room:Y, Kitchen:Y, B'fast:Y, WiFi:Y, Locker:Y, Recep:ltd; Note: bus pickup, bikes, minimart, luggage rm, laundry, tour desk, parking

Kelowna Okanagan Lake Hostel, 730 Bernard Ave, Kelowna, BC; *info@ kelownaolhostel.com/*, T:+1(778)484.5868; $24Bed, Pvt.room:Y, Kitchen:Y, B'fast:Y, WiFi:Y, Locker:N, Recep:ltd; Note: laundry, tour desk, parking, games, tea/coffee

NELSON is a town of 10,000 close to the US border. As such it received many US conscientious objectors to the Vietnam War in the '60's, who have since transformed the town. Once a silver-mining boom town, Nelson was faced with disaster when the forest products industry collapsed. They restored Baker Street to its former brilliance, and that is tourist silver these days... that and marijuana production. Hey, work's work.

WhiteHouse Backpackers Lodge, 816 Vernon St, Nelson, BC; T:+1(250)352.0505, *Info@ white-house.ca/*; $26Bed, Pvt.room:N, Kitchen:Y, B'fast:Y, WiFi:Y, Locker:Y, Recep:ltd; Note: nr G-H bus, bikes, parking, luggage room, Victorian house

PEMBERTON is a town of 2200, 2400 in the metro area J, that maintains its traditional Old West movie-set appearance. The Fraser Canyon Gold Rush came through here in 1858. Besides many trails for hiking, biking, and horse, there is agro-tourism, based on Pemberton's important seed-bank industry.

Hostel Shiloh_Works, Box 1304, Pemberton/Mt.Currie BC; *Info@ shiloh-works.com/*, T:+1(604)452.0196; $26Bed, Pvt.room:Y, Kitchen:Y, B'fast:N, WiFi:Y, Locker:Y, Recep:7a>10p; Note: backcountry, hot tub, billiards, parking

PENTICTON is a city of 43,000 in the Okanagan Valley of British Columbia. Fruit growing is important, including peaches and apples. Rock climbing is popular in this area, and there are beaches on the lake.

HI-Penticton, 464 Ellis St, Penticton, BC; *hihostels.ca/*, TF:1(866)782.9736, T:+1(250)492.3992; $26Bed, Pvt.room:Y, Kitchen:Y, B'fast:N, WiFi:Y, Locker:Y, Recep:8a/10p; Note: central, resto/bar, bikes, tour desk, wh/chair OK, luggage rm

POWELL RIVER is a town of 13,000 nestled among the fjords of the Georgia Strait that separate Vancouver Island from the mainland. Though part of the mainland, access is by ferry only. The pulp mill is downsizing; ecotourism is growing.

Powell River Harbour GH, 4454 Willingdon Ave, Powell River, BC; *prhostel.ca/*, TF:1(877)709.7700, *prhostel@gmail.com*; $39Bed, Pvt.room:Y, Kitchen:Y, B'fast:$, WiFi:Y, Locker:N, Recep:24/7; Note: resto, luggage room, parking, laundry

Higgin's Inn, 10150 Douglas Bay Rd, Powell River, BC; T:+1(604)487.1119, *rob@ higginsinn.ca/*;$26Bed, Pvt.room:Y, Kitchen:Y, B'fast:$, WiFi:Y, Locker:N, Recep:ltd; Note: wh/chair OK, laundry, arpt trans $

PRINCE GEORGE is a city of 71,000 (metro area 84K), nestled at the junction of the Fraser and Nechako Rivers, and highways 16 and 97, the self-described "northern capital of BC." Originally a center of fur-trading, followed by forestry, service industries now dominate. Mr. PG, composed of logs, is the slowly rotting town mascot.

Prince Georges Hostel (The Manor), 197 Quebec St, Prince George, BC; *Info@ princegeorgehostel.com/*, T:+1(250)900.9966; $20Bed, Pvt.room:Y, Kitchen:Y, B'fast:N, WiFi:Y, Locker:Y, Recep:ltd; Note: tour desk, luggage room

PRINCE RUPERT is a northern port city on the Pacific, with a population of 12,500. Fishing and forestry were traditionally important, activities now in sharp decline. A new container port and increased tourism give hope for the future. It is a cruise stop on the Inside Passage. The countryside has whales, eagles, and grizzlies.

Black Rooster Roadhouse Hostel, 501 - 6th Ave W, Prince Rupert, BC; T:+1(866)371.5337, *info@ blackrooster.ca/*; $27Bed, Pvt.room:Y, Kitchen:Y, B'fast:N, WiFi:Y, Locker:$, Recep:ltd; Note: laundry, luggage room $, parking, free pickup form ferry/bus/train

Pioneer Hostel Prince Rupert, 167-3rd Ave E, Prince Rupert, BC; *pioneerhostel.com/*, TF:1(888)794.9998, *pioneer@citytel.net*; $26Bed, Pvt.room:Y, Kitchen:Y, B'fast:N, WiFi:Y, Locker:Y, Recep:ltd; Note: wh/chair OK, shuttle, parking, luggage room, laundry, tea/coffee

REVELSTOKE is a town of 7000 in the eastern part of BC along the Canadian Pacific Railway, and somewhat closer to Alberta than Vancouver. The railroad is traditionally the chief employer, but Mt. Revelstoke National Park and the Mountain Resort are changing all that.

Revelstoke SameSun Backpacker, 400-2nd St West, Revelstoke, BC; *samesun.com/*, T:+1(250)837.4050, TF:1(877)972.6378; $28Bed, Pvt.room:Y, Kitchen:Y, B'fast:N, WiFi:Y, Locker:N, Recep:8a/10p; Note: bikes, billiards, parking, luggage room, basic

ROSSLAND is a town of 3500 up in the hills at 3350ft/1000mt in the Kootenay Region near the US border, and due north of Spokane. Did you know the Columbia comes up this way? Now you do. Founded in the Gold Rush of 1897, tourism lures now.

The Mountain Shadow Hostel, 2125 Columbia Ave, Rossland, BC; T:+1(250)362.7160, *info@ mshostel.com/*; $20Bed, Pvt.room:N, Kitchen:Y,

B'fast:N, WiFi:Y, Locker:Y, Recep:ltd; Note: tour desk, laundry, safe deposit, central

VANCOUVER is a city of more than 600,000, with almost four times that many in the metro area. More than half are not native English-speakers! Vancouver grew up in the Fraser gold rush of 1858, and the original settlement was called Gastown, now the bohemian part of town, featuring restaurants, bars and clubs and... more than a few transients and homeless people, flocking to the sunshine like birds come home to roost. The Klondike gold rush of 1898 kept dreams alive for the frontier area, and many Asians came to provide labor, setting the stage for the diversity of today. They also built some landmark buildings back then, some of them the skyscrapers of their day: the Carter-Cotton Building, the Dominion Building (1907) and the Sun Tower (1911).

Museums include the Vancouver Maritime Museum, the H. R. MacMillan Space Centre, the Vancouver Museum, and the Museum of Anthropology at UBC. Festivals include the PuSh International Performing Arts Festival in January, the Vancouver Fringe Festival in September, and the Vancouver International Film Festival. Vancouver is now 'Hollywood north' for film production. Granville is best for nightlife. Van-Town has some distinct ethnic neighborhoods: Chinatown, Punjabi Market, Little Italy, Greektown, and former Japantown. This is by far the best Chinatown — and Chinese food — north of San Fran. I walked there everyday from my digs in Gastown in 2006 for my daily sustenance. Vancouver is the warmest city in Canada (think Seattle). *Brrrr....*

Samesun Backpacker Lodge, 1018 Granville St, Vancouver, BC; *samesun.com/*, T:+1(604)682.8226, TF:1(877)972.6378; $29Bed, Pvt.room:Y, Kitchen:Y, B'fast:Y, WiFi:Y, Locker:Y, Recep:24/7; Note: resto/bar, billiards, party, luggage room, laundry, tour desk, central

Cambie Hostel Seymour (Downtown), 515 Seymour St, Vancouver, BC; T:+1(604)684.7757, *seymour@ thecambie.com/*, TF:1.866.623.8496;

Cambie Hostel Gastown, 300 Cambie St, Vancouver, BC; *gastown@ thecambie.com/*, T:+1(604)688.9158; $27Bed, Pvt.room:Y, Kitchen:Y, B'fast:Y, WiFi:Y, Locker:Y, Recep:24/7; Note: no locals, resto/bar, billiards, luggage room, bohemian Gastown

HI-Vancouver Downtown, 1114 Burnaby St; T:+1(604)684.4565

HI-Vancouver Jericho Beach, 1515 Discovery St; T:+1(604)224.3208

HI-Vancouver Central, 1025 Granville St, Vancouver, BC; *hihostels.ca/*, T:+1(604)685.5335; TF: 1.866.762.4122; $32Bed, Pvt.room:Y, Kitchen:N, B'fast:Y, WiFi:Y, Locker:Y, Recep:24/7; Note: pool, lift, tea/cof, luggage rm, laundry, tour desk

C&N B'packers (Central Stn), 1038 Main St; T:+1(604)681.9118

C&N Backpackers Hostel, 927 Main St, Vancouver, BC; T:+1(604)682.2441, *Info@ cnnbackpackers.com/*; $21Bed, Pvt.room:Y, Kitchen:N, B'fast:$, WiFi:Y, Locker:Y, Recep:8a>3a; Note: café, bikes, minimart, luggage room, tour desk, basic

St. Clair Hotel & Hostel, 577 Richards St, Vancouver, BC; T:+1(604)684.3713, *Info@ stclairvancouver.com/*; $26Bed, Pvt.room:Y, Kitchen:N, B'fast:N, WiFi:Y, Locker:N, Recep:>9p; Note: luggage room, laundry, Microwave, Kettle, Fridge

VANCOUVER ISLAND is the 43rd largest island in the world and 11th in Canada. Victoria is the largest city, with 80,000 inhabitants, and full of 19th century Victorian architecture. It is also known as the City of Gardens for its gentility and mild climate, which attracts a disproportionate number of retirees. Music festivals range from philharmonic to electronic. The British Columbia Parliament Buildings and Christ Church Cathedral are major landmarks, Chinatown and Fisherman's Wharf interesting excursions; sounds like San Fran. And, oh yeah, it is also the capital of BC... and as far away from the rest of it as can possibly be. There are ferry services from Victoria to Port Angeles, Seattle, and Bellingham, WA, and Vancouver City, BC.

Nanaimo is also a city of around 80K, and known for its bathtub racing, yep. It should be known for its Chinatowns, of which there have been four distinct ones. It is the main ferry hub for central Vancouver Island, with connections to Vancouver city and elsewhere. There is an underground music scene, blues festivals, and art and theatre events. Outside of the cities there are many old-growth forests, a bone of contention between loggers and environmentalists. Commercial fishing is still important, and tourist activities include sport fishing, whale-watching, scuba diving, hiking, and skiing. There are six ferry routes and services from points north on the island and mainland. The Georgia Strait between them is a marine highway. The Vancouver Island Range reaches a high point of 7200ft/2195mt.

Shantz Haus Hostel, 520-5 St, Courtenay, BC; *info@ shantzhostel.com/*, T:+1(250)703.2060; $23Bed, Pvt.room:N, Kitchen:Y, B'fast:N, WiFi:Y, Locker:Y, Recep:ltd; Note: downtown, fireplace, books

The Cona Hostel, 440 Anderton Ave, Courtenay, BC; T:+1(250)331.0991, *Info@ theconahostel.com/*; $26Bed, Pvt.room:N, Kitchen:Y, B'fast:N, WiFi:Y, Locker:N, Recep:8a/9p; Note: Mt. Washington, tour desk, luggage rm, laundry, games, downtown

Riding Fool Hostel, 2705 Dunsmuir Ave, Cumberland, BC; T:+1(250)336.8250, *Info@ ridingfool.com/*; $26Bed, Pvt.room:N, Kitchen:Y, B'fast:N, WiFi:Y, Locker:Y, Recep:9a/9p; Note: café, bikes, books, luggage room, tour desk, resto, billiards, Nature

Painted Turtle GH, 121 Bastion St, Nanaimo, BC; *stay@ paintedturtle.ca/*, T:+1(250)753.4432; $23Bed, Pvt.room:Y, Kitchen:Y, B'fast:N, WiFi:Y, Locker:Y, Recep:ltd; Note: historic bldg, bar, books, tour desk, laundry, luggage room

Tsunami Backpackers GH, 5779 River Rd, Vancouver Is, Pt. Alberni, BC; T:+1(250)724.9936, *tsunamibackpackers.hostel.com/*; $20Bed, Pvt.room:N, Kitchen:Y, B'fast:N, WiFi:Y, Locker:N, Recep:ltd; Note: billiards, parking, luggage room, laundry, tour desk, bakery, Nature

North Coast Trail Backpackers Ltd, 8635 Granville St, Port Hardy, BC; *northcoasthostel.ca/*, T:+1(250)949.9441; $24Bed, Pvt.room:Y, Kitchen:Y, B'fast:N, WiFi:Y, Locker:N, Recep:ltd; Note: camping, café, billiards, books, parking, luggage room, laundry, central

C&N Backpackers Hostel, 8740 Main, Port Hardy, BC; T:+1(250)949.3030, *Info@ cnnbackpackers.com*; $21Bed, Pvt.room:Y, Kitchen:Y, B'fast:N, WiFi:Y, Locker:N, Recep:24/7; Note: wh/chair OK, tour desk, parking, luggage room

C&N Backpackers– Ucluelet, 2081 Peninsula Rd, Ucluelet, BC; 250.726.7416

Tofino Travellers Guesthouse, 231 Main St, Tofino, BC; *stay@ tofinotravellers.com*, T:250.725.2338, *tofinotravellersguesthouse.com/*; $29Bed, Pvt. room:N, Kitchen:Y, B'fast:Y, WiFi:Y, Locker:N, Recep:ltd; Note: bikes, parking, luggage room, laundry, tour desk, wild west coast

Ocean Island Inn/Backpackers/Suites, 791 Pandora Ave, Victoria, BC; *oceanisland.com/*, T:+1(250)385.1788; $21Bed, Pvt.room:Y, Kitchen:Y, B'fast:$ WiFi:Y, Locker:Y, Recep:24/7; Note: historic bldg, resto/bar, luggage room, laundry, parking, tour desk

HI Victoria, 516 Yates St, Victoria, BC; TF:1.866.762.4122, *hihostels.ca/*, T:+1(250)385.4511; $21Bed, Pvt.room:N, Kitchen:Y, B'fast:N, WiFi:Y, Locker:Y,

Recep:24/7; Note: wh/chair OK, billiards, luggage room, laundry, tour desk, maps

The Turtle Hostel, 1608 Quadra St, Victoria, BC; *turtlehostel.ca/*, T/F:+1(250)381.3210, *turtle.hostel@gmail.com*; $20Bed, Pvt.room:Y, Kitchen:Y, B'fast:N, WiFi:Y, Locker:Y, Recep:ltd; Note: luggage room $, laundry, parking, central, basic

VERNON is a city of almost 40,000 (city proper, half again that many in the metro area), in the south-central Okanagan region of BC. There is a Winter Carnival in that season, a Sunshine festival for summer, the Komasket music festival and a Creative Chaos arts fair, one of the city's highlights.

Silver Star SameSun Ski Lodge, 9898 Pinnacles Rd, Silver Star, BC; T:+1(250)545.8933, *samesun.com/*, TF:1.877.9.SAMESUN; $35Bed, Pvt.room:N, Kitchen:Y, B'fast:Y, WiFi:Y, Locker:Y, Recep:ltd; Note: arpt trans, billiards, luggage room, laundry, parking

WHISTLER is a resort town of almost 10,000 some 80mi/130km north of Vancouver. There are winter sports in the winter, summer sports in the summer, good enough for the Winter Olympics in 2010. There are bus, rail, and air connections,

Fireside Lodge, 2117 Nordic Dr, Whistler, BC; *info@ firesidelodge.org/*, TF:1.866.932.3994; $26Bed, Pvt.room:Y, Kitchen:Y, B'fast:N, WiFi:Y, Locker:N, Recep:8a/8p; Note: billiards, books, laundry, luggage room, terrace, games

HI Whistler, 1035 Legacy Way, Whistler, BC; TF:1.866.762.4122, *hihostels.ca/*, T:+1(604)962.0025; $32Bed, Pvt.room:Y, Kitchen:Y, B'fast:$, WiFi:Y, Locker:Y, Recep:24/7; Note: wh/chair OK, billiards, luggage room, laundry, resto/bar, bikes, far

Southside Lodge, 2102 Lake Placid Rd, Whistler, BC; *southsidelodge.com/*, T:+1(604)932.3644; $26Bed, Pvt.room:N, Kitchen:Y, B'fast:$, WiFi:Y, Locker:Y, Recep:8p; Note: @bus stn, arpt trans, resto/bar, minimart, laundry, luggage room

UBC Whistler Lodge, 2124 Nordic Dr, Whistler, BC; TF:1(877)932.6604, *whistler@ ams.ubc.ca/*; T:+1(604)822.5851; $29Bed, Pvt.room:N, Kitchen:Y, B'fast:N, WiFi:Y, Locker:Y, Recep:ltd; Note: laundry, parking, billiards, hot tub, curtains no doors

37) Manitoba

CHURCHILL is a town of less than 1000 people on the shores of Hudson Bay in Manitoba. At fifty-eight degrees north latitude — lower than Anchorage, or Oslo — this is possibly the most southerly point in the world where polar bears can be seen, best in late fall. Beluga whales come in summer; so do birds, more than 100 species. It's cold.

Tundra House Hostel, 51 Frankin St, Churchill, MB; *hostel@ tundrainn. com/*, TF:1(800)265.8563; $36Bed, Pvt.room:Y, Kitchen:Y, B'fast:N, WiFi:Y, Locker:Y, Recep:24/7; Note: resto/bar, books, tour desk, luggage rm, laundry

38) New Brunswick

MIRAMICHI is a city of 18,000 once known for its shipbuilding, and still based primarily on mining, forestry, and fishing. There is substantial folklore, based on the traditional Mi'kmaq, Acadian, and Scotch-Irish culture, and expressed in the Miramichi Folksong Festival, pow-wows of the nearby Eel Ground First Nation and Metepenagiag Mi'kmaq Nation, La Fête nationale des Acadiens, Miramichi Scottish Festival, and more.

The Officers Quarters Hostel, 15 Cole Crescent, Miramichi, NB;*the-officers-quarters.com/*, T:+1(250)753.4173, *TheHostel@rogers.com*; $19Bed, Pvt. room:Y, Kitchen:Y, B'fast:Y, WiFi:Y, Locker:N, Recep:ltd; Note: billiards, luggage rm, tour desk, parking, laundry

MONCTON is a city of 70,000 and one of Canada's most bilingual, almost 50-50. They use it, too, with bilingual call centers employing almost 5000. Tourist attractions are mostly of the mass-market amusement-park variety, though there are concert venues and brew pubs (burp). C U at the Pump House.

C'mon Inn Hostel, 47 Fleet St, Moncton, NB; *monctonhostel.ca/*, T:+1(506)854.8155, *monctonhostel@yahoo.ca*; $26Bed, Pvt.room:Y, Kitchen:Y, B'fast:Y, WiFi:Y, Locker:Y, Recep:9a>9p; Note: historic house, luggage room, tour desk, parking, central

ST. JOHN ('Fundy City,' not to be confused with St. John's, NL) is the largest city of New Brunswick in the eastern Maritime Provinces, with a population of 70,000, and twice that in the metro area. The Reversing Falls are created by rising tides in the narrow gorge where the St. John River joins the Bay of Fundy. There are thirteen historic sites.

Newman House Hostel, 60 Newman St, St. John, NB; *newmanhousehostel@ gmail.com*; T:+1(506)635.8461; $28Bed, Pvt.room:Y, Kitchen:Y, B'fast:Y, WiFi:Y, Locker:N, Recep:ltd; Note: linen fee, parking, homestay, central, wh/chair OK

39) Newfoundland and Labrador

ST. JOHN'S, (not to be confused with St. John, NB) is the capital and largest city — pop. 200,000 — of Newfoundland and Labrador. Founded in 1497, and permanently settled before 1620, it is often considered the oldest English settlement on the continent. Where the cod fields have failed recently, proximity to nearby oil fields is taking up the slack. Architecture is unique and brightly colored. Nightlife is good, museums many.

HI-St. John's (City Hostel), 18 Gower St, St. John's, NL; *hihostels.ca/*, T:+1(709)754.4789; $34Bed, Pvt.room:Y, Kitchen:Y, B'fast:N, WiFi:Y, Locker:Y, Recep:24/7; Note: bikes, books, parking, luggage room, laundry, tour desk, games

TRINITY EAST is a tiny fishing village that features puffins, whales, kayaks and trails.

Skerwink Hostel, Trinity East, Newfoundland; T:+1(709)557.2015, *manager@ skerwinkhostel.com*; $16Bed, Pvt.room:Y, Kitchen:Y, B'fast:Y, WiFi:Y, Locker:N, Recep:24/7; Note: seasonal, camping OK, wheelchair OK, bikes, tour desk, parking

40) Nova Scotia

CALEDONIA is a town in the far eastern Canadian province of Nova Scotia, about 30 mi/50km north of Liverpool, and 11mi/18km from the main entrance to Kejimkujik National Park. It is the major village in the area known as North Queens, with a population of approximately 1500.

Caledonia Country Hostel, 9960 Nova Scotia Trunk 8, Caledonia, NS; *kejihostel.wordpress.com/*, T:+1(902)682.3266, *info@caledoniacountryhostel.com*; $31Bed, Pvt.room:N, Kitchen:Y, B'fast:Y, WiFi:Y, Locker:N, Recep:ltd; Note: natl park, camping OK, parking, bikes, Tango Shuttle

CAPE BRETON is the most eastern point of Nova Scotia, an island connected to the mainland by artificial causeway. It is known for its fiddle music brought by Scottish immigrants (Scotia, get it?). Judique has a Celtic Music Interpretive Centre.

Cabot Trail Hostel, 23349 Cabot Trail, Cape Breton Is, NS; *pam.otoole@ cabottrailhostel.com/*, T:+1(877)776.0707; $29Bed, Pvt.room:Y, Kitchen:Y, B'fast:N, WiFi:Y, Locker:N, Recep:ltd; Note: bikes, parking, luggage rm, wh/chair OK, tea/coffee

Bear On The Lake G/House, 10705 Hwy. 105, bet. Whycocomagh & Baddec; T:+1(902)756.2750, *Info@ bearonthelake.com/*, TF:866.718.5253; $27Bed,

Pvt.room:Y, Kitchen:Y, B'fast:N, WiFi:Y, Locker:N, Recep:ltd; Note: parking, luggage rm, laundry, tour desk, Nature

DIGBY is a town of a couple thousand on the western end of Nova Scotia and known as the "Scallop Capital of the World." There is a festival to celebrate its history in August and a major motorcycle rally on Labor Day weekend.

Digby Backpackers Inn, 168 Queen St, Digby, NS; T:+1(902)245.4573, *Info@ digbyhostel.com/*; $31Bed, Pvt.room:Y, Kitchen:Y, B'fast:Y, WiFi:Y, Locker:N, Recep:>9p; Note: cash only, bikes, parking, tour desk, laundry, c.c. OK

HALIFAX, once a simple city, is now a regional municipality of 400K, capital of the province. There are historic buildings in the urban core. Argyle Street is a cool place to chill. The Atlantic Film Festival, Halifax Busker Festival, Greekfest, Atlantic Jazz Festival, and the Multicultural Festival are notable events.

HI Halifax - Heritage House Hostel, 1253 Barrington St, Halifax, NS; *hihostels.ca/*, T:+1(902)422.3863; $31Bed, Pvt.room:N, Kitchen:Y, B'fast:N, WiFi:Y, Locker:Y, Recep:ltd; Note: tour desk, luggage room, parking

Halifax Backpackers, 2193 Gottingen St, Halifax, NS; T:+1(902)431.3170, *Info@ halifaxbackpackers.com/*; $23Bed, Pvt.room:N, Kitchen:Y, B'fast:N, WiFi:Y, Locker:N, Recep:8a>8p; Note: cafe, tour desk, luggage room, basic

MAHONE BAY is a town on the bay of the same name, and known for its wooden boat building. The bay is known for its innumerable small islands. The Acadians lost a major battle with the English here in 1756 before being deported to y'all-know-where.

Kip/Kaboodle M. Bay/Lunenburg YH, 9466 #3 Hwy RR1, Mahone Bay, NS; T:+1(902)531.5494, *Info@ kiwikaboodle.com/*, TF:1(866)0549.4522; $31Bed, Pvt.room:Y, Kitchen:N, B'fast:N, WiFi:Y, Locker:Y, Recep:ltd; Note: south shore NS, bikes, luggage rm, tour desk, parking

41) Ontario

ALGONQUIN PARK is a provincial park in central Ontario province covering some 2950sq.mi/7650sq.km. Located on a Greyhound bus route, it is accessible to both Ottawa and Toronto, Hwy. 60 running through the south and the Trans-Canada highway passing to the north. There are more than 2400 lakes, forests, and wildlife.

Algonquin Backpackers, 32990 Hwy 62, Algonquin Park, ON, *algonquinbackpacker.com/*, TF:1.800.595.8064, *booking@TheArlington.ca*; $25Bed, Pvt.room:Y, Kitchen:Y, B'fast:N, WiFi:Y, Locker:N, Recep:24/7; Note: bar, parking, luggage rm, laundry, tour desk

Algonquin's Wolf Den Bunkhouse, 4568 Hwy 60, Oxtongue Lake, Algonquin;

T:1+(705)635.WDEN(9336), *wden@ wolfdenbunkhouse.com/*; $26Bed, Pvt. room:Y, Kitchen:Y, B'fast:N, WiFi:N, Locker:N, Recep:24/7; Note: on a Greyhound bus route, parking, tour desk, safe deposit

HAMILTON is a city of over 700,000 in its metro area, and highly industrialized. Recently there has been a growing arts movement, and a return to revitalize the downtown core.

Hamilton Guesthouse, 158 Mary St, Hamilton, ON; *hamiltonguesthouse. info/*, T:+1(289)396.1659, *hamilton.guesthouse@gmail.com*; $21Bed, Pvt.room:Y, Kitchen:Y, B'fast:N, WiFi:Y, Locker:N, Recep:>11p; Note: tea/coffee, luggage room, parking, c.c.

MANITOULIN ISLAND is a major island of over 12,500 people on Lake Huron. It is popular for tourism in summer. There is a prehistoric archeological site. The Beaver Wars were once fought here over the fur trade. There is a ferry and a one-lane bridge.

Auberge Inn, 71 McNevin St, Providence Bay, Manitoulin Island, ON; *Info@ aubergeinn.ca/*, T:+1(705)377.4392; $40Bed, Pvt.room:Y, Kitchen:N, B'fast:Y, WiFi:Y, Locker:Y, Recep:ltd; Note: café, bikes, luggage room, parking

NIAGARA FALLS is a city of 83,000 along that narrow coccyx that joins southern Canada to the northern US at the small of the back, and famous for that huge bladder of water spilling from Lake Erie to Lake Ontario so precipitously as to attract millions of visitors to come each year to view the spectacle. And that they do, the Canadian side with the best view of both falls — Niagara and Horseshoe — and the casinos, trinket shops, and neon signs to make sure you don't forget you're a tourist. Sometimes it's nice to be American.

Niagara Falls Backpackers Hostel, 4219 Huron St, Niagara Falls, ON; *backpackers.ca/*, T:+1(905)357.4266, *niagarafallshostel@hotmail.com*; $26Bed, Pvt. room:Y, Kitchen:Y, B'fast:Y, WiFi:Y, Locker:Y, Recep:24/7; Note: tour desk, parking, luggage room, forex

HI Niagara Falls Hostel, 4549 Cataract Ave, Niagara Falls, ON; *hihostels. com/*, T:+1(905)357.0770, *info@hostellingniagara.com*; $29Bed, Pvt.room:Y, Kitchen:Y, B'fast:Y, WiFi:Y, Locker:Y, Recep:ltd; Note: bikes, billiards, books, tour desk, parking, luggage room, laundry

ACBB Hostel Niagara, 5741 McGrail Ave, Niagara Falls, ON; T:+1(905)359.4815, (see FB page); $31Bed, Pvt.room:Y, Kitchen:Y, B'fast:Y, WiFi:Y, Locker:N, Recep:ltd; Note: wh/chair OK, luggage room, laundry, safe deposit, near falls

OTTAWA is the capital of the country, of course, and its fourth-largest city, with a population of almost 1.5 million in the greater metro area. The Rideau Canal is the oldest continuously operated one in North America, a world heritage site. There are twenty-four other national historic sites here, too. It has Canada's largest festival, Winterlude, plus many others, such as Bluesfest, Canadian Tulip Festival, Ottawa Dragon Boat Festival, Ottawa International Jazz Festival, Fringe Festival and Folk Music Festival; not bad for government work.

HI - Ottawa Jail Hostel, 75 Nicholas St, Ottawa, ON; T:+1(613)235.2595, *ottawa.jail@ hihostels.ca/*; $28Bed, Pvt.room:Y, Kitchen:Y, B'fast:Y, WiFi:Y, Locker:Y, Recep:ltd; Note: bar, tour desk, parking, luggage room, central

Ottawa Backpackers Inn, 203 York St, Ottawa, ON; T:+1(613)241.3402, *Info@ ottawahostel.com/*; $23Bed, Pvt.room:Y, Kitchen:Y, B'fast:$, WiFi:Y, Locker:Y, Recep:8a>12m; Note: café, parking, luggage room, laundry

Barefoot Hostel, 455 Cumberland St, Ottawa, ON; *bfh@ barefoothostel.com/*, T:+1(613)237.0335; $35Bed, Pvt.room:N, Kitchen:Y, B'fast:N, WiFi:Y, Locker:Y, Recep:>11p; Note: no smoke, no shoes (barefoot, get it?), cozy, central

TORONTO is Canada's largest city, with a population of more than 2.5 million in the city proper, twice that in the metro area. Half of that population was born outside of Canada! That's a lot of diversity. There are a lot of high-rises, too, both residential and commercial. Some of the more interesting neighborhoods are, in fact, the ethnic ones, such as the two Chinatowns, the Greektown area, Little Italy, Portugal Village, and Little India, among others. Prime tourist destinations include the Royal Ontario Museum, the Toronto Zoo, the Art Gallery of Ontario, the Gardiner Museum of ceramic art, theOntario Science Centre, the Bata Shoe Museum, and Textile Museum of Canada.

Canadiana Backpackers Inn, 42 Widmer St, Toronto, ON; T:+1(416)598.8940, *Info@ canadianalodging.com/*; $23Bed, Pvt.room:Y, Kitchen:Y, B'fast:Y, WiFi:Y, Locker:Y, Recep:24/7; Note: arpt trans, billiards, forex, parking, luggage room, laundry, tour desk

The Only Backpacker's Inn, 968 Danforth Ave, Toronto, ON; TF:1(855)463.3249, *backpackers@ theonlycafe.com/*, T:+1(416)463.3249; $25Bed, Pvt.room:N, Kitchen:Y, B'fast:Y, WiFi:Y, Locker:Y, Recep:ltd; Note: Greek town, nr metro, resto/bar, luggage room, laundry, tea/coffee

Planet Traveler, 357 College St, Toronto, ON; *theplanettraveler.com/*, T:+1(647)352.8747, *planettravelerhostel@gmail.com*; $31Bed, Pvt.room:Y, Kitchen:Y, B'fast:Y, WiFi:Y, Locker:Y, Recep:ltd; Note: café, bikes, books, parking, luggage room, laundry, eco-friendly

All Days Hostel, 5 Selby St, Toronto, ON; T:+1(647)955.2601, *Info@ alldayshostel.com/*; $31Bed, Pvt.room:Y, Kitchen:Y, B'fast:N, WiFi:Y, Locker:Y, Recep:24/7; Note: parking, luggage room, laundry, forex, safe dep.

HI-Toronto YH, 76 Church St, Toronto, ON; *toronto@ hihostels.ca*, T:+1(416)971.4440; $23Bed, Pvt.room:Y, Kitchen:Y, B'fast:$, WiFi:Y, Locker:Y, Recep:24/7; Note: downtown, café, lift, luggage room, laundry, tour desk, tea/coffee

The Clarence Park, 7 Clarence Sq, Toronto, ON; T:+1(647)498.7070, *Info@ theclarencepark.com*; $26Bed, Pvt.room:Y, Kitchen:Y, B'fast:$, WiFi:Y, Locker:Y, Recep:ltd; Note: café, parking, luggage room, laundry, central

Global Village Kensington, 280 Augusta St, Toronto, ON; *globalvillagekensington.com/*, TF:1(866)663.2093; $26Bed, Pvt.room:Y, Kitchen:Y, B'fast:N, WiFi:Y, Locker:Y, Recep:ltd; Note: pool, resto, minimart, tour desk, luggage, basic

Global Village Backpackers - Toronto, 460 King St W, Toronto, ON; T:+1(416)703.8540, *info@ globalbackpackers.com/*; $25Bed, Pvt.room:Y, Kitchen:Y, B'fast:Y, WiFi:Y, Locker:Y, Recep:24/7; Note: bar/club, billiards, luggage room, laundry, tour desk, ATM, central

42) Prince Edward Island

CHARLOTTETOWN is the capital and largest city of Prince Edward Island, which lies parallel to the coasts of New Brunswick and Nova Scotia in Canada's far east. It has a population of 32,000, twice that in the metro area. It is a transportation and technology hub, and includes a historic district, with eleven historic sites.

HI Charlottetown Backpackers Inn, 60 Hillsborough St, Charlottetown, PE; T:+1(902)367.5749, *Info@ charlottetownbackpackers.com/*; $33Bed, Pvt. room:Y, Kitchen:N, B'fast:Y, WiFi:Y, Locker:N, Recep:ltd; Note: seasonal, bikes, billiards, parking

43) Quebec

FORILLON NATIONAL PARK (GASPE) was Quebec's first national park, located far out on the tip of the Gaspe Peninsula. There are forests, coast, marshes, dunes, cliffs, and the last gasp of the Appalachians, full of sea birds, whales, seals, black bears,moose, and more. Gaspe' is served by bus, rail, and air.

Auberge Griffon Aventure, 829 Boulevard Griffon, Gaspé, QC; *aubergegaspe.com/*, T:+1(418)360.6614; *info@griffonaventure;* $26Bed, Pvt. room:N, Kitchen:Y, B'fast:N, WiFi:Y, Locker:N, Recep:ltd; Note: resto/bar, billiards, parking, luggage room, tour desk, bikes

Auberge Internationale Forillon, 2095 Boul. de Grande Greve, Gaspé, QC; T:+1(418)892.5153, *aubergeinternationaleforillon.com/*; $31Bed, Pvt.room:N, Kitchen:Y, B'fast:N, WiFi:Y, Locker:Y, Recep:ltd; Note: resto/bar, wh/chair OK, parking, luggage rm, tour desk, arpt pickup

Auberge Jeunesse La Merluche, 202 Rue de la Reine, Gaspe QC; *auberge@ lamerluche.com/,* T:+1(418)368.8000; $30Bed, Pvt.room:Y, Kitchen:Y, B'fast:N, WiFi:Y, Locker:Y, Recep:>10p; Note: arpt trans, tour desk, luggage room, wh/ chair OK, lift, bikes, laundry

MATANE is a city of almost 15K on the south shore of the St. Lawrence Seaway in Quebec. It is first stop on Gaspe Peninsula's tourist circuit. Shrimp here are renowned.

There is ferry service.

Aub/Jeun Du Manoir Des Sapins, 180 boul. Perron Sainte-Felicite, Matane, QC; *Info@ manoirdessapins.com/,* T:+1(418)733.8182; $23Bed, Pvt. room:Y, Kitchen:Y, B'fast:$, WiFi:Y, Locker:N, Recep:24/7; Note: veg/organic meals, parking, laundry

MONT-TREMBLANT is a city of 9500 almost equidistant — 85mi/135km — from Montreal and Ottawa. It is famous for its ski resorts and other outdoor activities.

HI-Mont-Tremblant YH, 2213 Chemin du Village, Mont-Tremblant, QC; *hostellingtremblant.com/*, T:+1(819)425.6008; $25Bed, Pvt.room:Y, Kitchen:Y, B'fast:$, WiFi:Y, Locker:N, Recep:ltd; Note: café/bar, bikes, billiards, luggage room, tour desk, parking, laundry

MONTREAL is the largest city of Quebec province and second-largest in the country, with a population approaching two million in the city proper, and twice that in the metro area. Happily it still has a small-town feel to it, and is eminently walkable. It is also the second-largest French-speaking city in the world, and one of the few Western cities that is truly bilingual. Ironically it wasn't intended that way, as Montreal was originally part of British North America, and by 1860 clearly its most important city. The politics of the 1970's and the Parti Quebecois changed all that, and resulted in Toronto's rise in commercial importance while Montreal declined, at the same time that Montreal was gaining increased international exposure with Expo '67 and Olympics '76. Things are calmer now, and Montreal assumes its rightful place as a bi-cultural capital.

Montreal is one of the few big cities north of the Rio Grande where the past is still present, and visible in the architecture, with fifty historic sites, in fact. Foremost among them are the Notre-Dame de Montréal Basilica, Bonsecours Market, and the banks on St. James Street. The Université de Montréal main building, Place Ville Marie office tower, and Olympic Stadium are more modern landmarks. The old historic district also includes the Old Port of Montreal, Place Jacques-Cartier, Montreal City Hall, Place d'Armes,

Pointe-à-Callière Museum, and the Montreal Science Centre. Mount Royal is a huge greenspace. Festivals include the Just for Laughs comedy festival, the Montreal International Jazz Festival, Montreal World Film Festival, Les FrancoFolies de Montréal, Nuits d'Afrique, Pop Montreal, and the Montreal Fireworks Festival. Given its European orientation, it's not surprising that there are many hostels. You might even find one by window-shopping.

HI-Montréal, 1030 Mackay St, Montréal, Quebec; TF:1(866)843.3317, *hihostels.ca/*, T:(514)843.3317; $22Bed, Pvt.room:Y, Kitchen:Y, B'fast:$, WiFi:Y, Locker:Y, Recep:ltd; Note: resto/bar, billiards, luggage rm, parking, laundry, books, nr metro

Montreal Central, 1586 Rue Saint-Hubert, Montreal, QC; T:+1(514)843.5739, *Info@ hostelmontrealcentral.com/*; $21Bed, Pvt.room:Y, Kitchen:Y, B'fast:Y, WiFi:Y, Locker:Y, Recep:24/7; Note: Latin Qtr, bar, bikes, books, luggage rm, tour desk, parking, laundry

Auberge De Paris Backpackers Hostel, 901 Rue Sherbrooke E, Montreal, QC; *Info@ aubergemontreal.com/*, T:+1(544)522.6124; $18Bed, Pvt.room:N, Kitchen:Y, B'fast:N, WiFi:Y, Locker:N, Recep:24/7; Note: luggage room, tea/ coffee, TV, books

Alexandrie Montréal, 1750 Rue Amherst, Montreal, QC; T:+1(514)525.9420, *alexandrie-montreal.com/*; $15Bed, Pvt.room:Y, Kitchen:Y, B'fast:Y, WiFi:Y, Locker:N, Recep:ltd; Note: nr metro/bus, tea/coffee, tour desk, parking, laundry

M Montreal, 1245 Rue St-Andre, Montreal, QC, *Info@ m-montreal.com/*, T:1(800)465.2929; $18Bed, Pvt.room:Y, Kitchen:Y, B'fast:Y, WiFi:Y, Locker:Y, Recep:24/7; Note: bar, billiards, books, tour desk, parking, luggage room, tea/coffee

Le Jazz Saint-Denis, 2099 Saint-Denis Rue, Montreal, QC; *stdenis@ jazzhostels.com/*, T:+1(514)448.4848; $19Bed, Pvt.room:Y, Kitchen:Y, B'fast:Y, WiFi:Y, Locker:Y, Recep:24/7; Note: luggage room, TV, a/c, central, nr metro, *tres Francais*

Hostel Chez Jean Montréal, 4136 Ave. Henri Julien, Montréal, QC; T:+1(514)843.8279, *aubergechezjean.com/*; $23Bed, Pvt.room:Y, Kitchen:Y, B'fast:Y, WiFi:Y, Locker:N, Recep:24/7; Note: café, bikes, forex, tour desk, parking, luggage rm

Le Gîte Du Parc Lafontaine, 1250 Sherbrooke East; T:+1(514)5223910;

Le Gite Du Plateau Mont Royal, 185 Rue Sherbrooke Est, Montreal, QC; T:+1(514)284.1276, *Info@ hostelmontreal.com/*; $29Bed, Pvt.room:Y, Kitchen:Y, B'fast:Y, WiFi:Y, Locker:Y, Recep:24/7; Note: Latin Qtr, books, forex, tour desk, laundry, luggage room, safe dep

Auberge-alternative, 358 Saint-Pierre Rue, Montreal, QC; T:+1(514)282.8069, *Info@ auberge-alternative.qc.ca/*; $27Bed, Pvt.room:N, Kitchen:Y, B'fast:Y, WiFi:Y, Locker:Y, Recep:ltd; Note: café, books, tour desk, laundry, luggage room, art

Gite Le Clic, 3953 Rue de Bullion, Montreal, QC; T+1(514)296.7905, *Info@ giteleclic.com/*; $23Bed, Pvt.room:Y, Kitchen:Y, B'fast:N, WiFi:Y, Locker:N, Recep:24/7; Note: café, laundry, luggage room, coffee/tea, basic

GoodLife Hostel, 650 Boul. de Maisonneuve Ouest #500, Montreal, QC; T:+1(514)501.6091, *facebook.com/GoodLifeHostel/*; $26Bed, Pvt.room:Y, Kitchen:Y, B'fast:N, WiFi:Y, Locker:Y, Recep:>10p; Note: historic bldg, nr bus/metro, forex, c.c.

Globetrotter Montreal, 1304 Ave. du Mont-Royal Est, Montreal, QC; T:+1(514)521.9628, *hostelglobetrotter.com/*; $20Bed, Pvt.room:Y, Kitchen:Y, B'fast:N, WiFi:Y, Locker:Y, Recep:>9p; Note: 2N min, midday lockout, café, pool, laundry, luggage rm, not central

Auberge L'Apéro, 1425 Rue Mackay, Montreal, QC; *paul@aubergeapero. com*, T:+1(514)316.1052, *facebook.com/aubergeapero/*; $20Bed, Pvt.room:N, Kitchen:Y, B'fast:Y, WiFi:Y, Locker:Y, Recep:ltd; Note: central, laundry, luggage rm, tour desk

Appartement Qualitas, 2146 Montgomery (2nd balc), Montreal, QC; T:+1(514)448.4060, *apartmentqualitas.com/*; $23Bed, Pvt.room:Y, Kitchen:Y, B'fast:$, WiFi:Y, Locker:N, Recep:9a>9p; Note: 3N min, cash only, meals, bikes, parking, TV, laundry, eco-friendly

QUEBEC is the capital of the province of the same name, and, with a population of over half a million (and half again as many in the metro area), is its second-largest, after Montreal. Unlike fully bilingual Montreal, only 145mi/230km to the southwest, Quebec is predominantly francophone. And founded by Champlain in 1608, it is the oldest American city north of Mexico. The old city is now a world heritage site. Landmarks here include the Château Frontenac hotel, the National Assembly of Quebec, the *Musée national des beaux-arts du Québec*, and the *Musée de la civilisation*.

HI-Québec City, 19, rue Ste-Ursule, Québec, QC; TF:1(866)694.0950, *hihostels.ca/*, T:+1(418)694.0755; $23Bed, Pvt.room:Y, Kitchen:Y, B'fast:$, WiFi:Y, Locker:Y, Recep:24/7; Note: historic bldg, resto/bar, billiards, luggage room, laundry, old town

Auberge De Jeunesse Maeva Quebec, 671 Rue Saint-Francois, Quebec, QC; *aubergemaeva.com/*, T:+1(418)914.9578; $24Bed, Pvt.room:N, Kitchen:Y,

B'fast:N, WiFi:Y, Locker:Y, Recep:9a/9p; Note: cash only, maps, tea/coffee, luggage room, nr bus/old town

La Belle Planete Backpacker Hostel, 386 Rue du Pont, Quebec, QC; *planetebackpackers.com/*, T:+1(418)264.4615, *quebechostel@gmail.com*; $23Bed, Pvt.room:Y, Kitchen:Y, B'fast:$, WiFi:Y, Locker:Y, Recep:>9p; Note: resto/bar, minimart, forex, gym, books, laundry, luggage room

RIVIERE-DU-LOUP is a town of almost 20,000 situated on the south shore of the St. Lawrence River in Quebec. There is a ferry across the river.

Auberge Intl Rivière Du Loup, 46 de l'Hôtel-de-Ville Rue, Rivière-du-Loup; *reservation@ aubergerdl.ca/*, T:+1(418)862.7566; $29Bed, Pvt.room:Y, Kitchen:N, B'fast:Y, WiFi:Y, Locker:N, Recep:ltd; Note: wh/chair Ok, bikes, tour desk, laundry, meals

SAGUENAY (CHICOUTIMI) is a city created in 2002, which included the former city of Chicoutimi, population 60,000, as one of its boroughs. Outdoor activities are good, both summer and winter.

Aub/Jeun Saguenay La Maison Price, 110 Rue Price Ouest, Chicoutimi, QC; TF:+1(877)549.0676, *Info@ ajsaguenay.com/*; $27Bed, Pvt.room:Y, Kitchen:Y, B'fast:Y, WiFi:Y, Locker:N, Recep:8a>5p; Note: resto/bar, minimart, hot tub, bikes, parking, luggage rm

Le Mains Tissees, 7643 Chemin des Chutes, La Baie, Saguenay, QC; T:+1(418)544.4456, *info@ lesmainstissees.com/*; $29Bed, Pvt.room:Y, Kitchen:Y, B'fast:N, WiFi:Y, Locker:Y, Recep:24/7; Note: arpt pickup, parking

SAINTE-ANNE-DES-MONTS is a small city of 7000 on the south shore of the St. Lawrence estuary. Tourism and fishing are the main industries. There are moose and caribou, last herd left south of the river. Gaspesie National Park and Chic-Choc Mountains are near.

Auberge Festive Sea Shack, 292 Boul Perron Est, Sainte-Anne-des-Monts, QC; T:+1(866)963.2999, *Info@ aubergefestive.com/*; $31Bed, Pvt.room:N, Kitchen:Y, B'fast:$, WiFi:Y, Locker:N, Recep:24/7; Note: resto/bar, hot tub, wh/chair OK, minimart, luggage room, parking

TEMISCOUATA is a town of 5000 on the lake of the same name on the south side of the St. Lawrence River. It was formed in 2010 from the merger of Cabano and Notre-Dame-du-Lac.

Temiscouata Intl Hostel, 788 Rue Commerciale N, Témiscouata-sur-le-Lac, QC; TF:1(888)688.1149, *info@ hostel@ aubergeinternationale. com/*; $28Bed, Pvt.room:Y, Kitchen:Y, B'fast:Y, WiFi:Y, Locker:Y, Recep:ltd; Note: wh/chair OK, café, pool, billiards, luggage room, laundry, parking

TROIS RIVIERES is a city of 150,000 halfway between Montreal and Quebec City. As the name ("three rivers") would suggest, this is a conjunction of waters, where the St. Maurice River meets the St. Lawrence. It was founded in 1634, second after Quebec City. Boulevard des Forges is the main drag, sometimes a pedestrian mall. There are festivals of music, poetry, and dance. Sounds good to me; guess I should have stopped.

HI-Trois-Rivières, 497 Radisson Rue, Trois-Rivières, QC; *hihostels.ca/*, T:+1(819)378.8010; $25Bed, Pvt.room:Y, Kitchen:Y, B'fast:$, WiFi:Y, Locker:Y, Recep:8a/9p; Note: café, bikes, parking, luggage room, laundry, downtown, tour info

44) Saskatchewan

REGINA is Saskatchewan's capital and second-largest city. Festivals in or near Regina through the year include the Cathedral Village Arts Festival; the Craven Country Jamboree; the Regina Folk Festival; the Regina Dragon Boat Festival; and Mosaic. Much of the city's original architecture was demolished, until preservation became popular.

HI-Regina, 2310 McIntyre St, Regina, Saskatchewan; TF:1(800)467.8357, *hihostels.ca/*, T:+1(306)791.8165; $36Bed, Pvt.room:N, Kitchen:Y, B'fast:N, WiFi:Y, Locker:Y, Recep:8a/10p; Note: advise late arrival, tour desk, luggage room, parking

45) Yukon Territory

WHITEHORSE is a city of twenty-something thousand at the end of a long road coming up through Canada. It's the start of a long road if you're going up to Dawson, even farther to Inuvik; better top up, and carry an extra tank. I met more than one person awaiting motorcycle parts here in 2011. At sixty degrees north latitude, your chances of seeing the aurora are pretty good, but not in summer. They say there are twenty hours of daylight then, but that sounds like a stretch; twilight maybe. A lesser-known excursion is down to Sitka, Alaska, with incredible scenery at the border area.

Lead Dog Backpacker, 5051-5th Ave, Whitehorse, YT; *Info@ leaddoginn. com/*, T:+1(867)456.2722; $34Bed, Pvt.room:N, Kitchen:Y, B'fast:N, WiFi:Y, Locker:N, Recep:24/7; Note: laundry, parking, tea/coffee, maps, central

The Beez Kneez Bakpakers Hostel, 408 Hoge St, Whitehorse, YT; *bzkneez. com/*, T:+1(867)456.2333, *hostel@klondiker.com*; $31Bed, Pvt.room:N, Kitchen:Y, B'fast:N, WiFi:Y, Locker:Y, Recep:8a>11p; Note: laundry, luggage room, parking, tea/coffee, books, maps

Part III: Mexico

Mexico is a Spanish-speaking nation of 113 million people, thirteenth largest and eleventh most populous in the world. Its history is longer than those of the USA or Canada, going all the way back to the earliest days of Spanish exploration, which landed on Mexican shores in 1519 and proceded to conquer. Mexico at that time was home to many advanced cultures — Aztec, Maya, Mixtec, and Zapotec — inheritors of traditions long ago passed down from the Olmecs, Teotihuacanos, and Toltecs. The Spaniards founded their Mexican capital right on top of the old one in 1524 and the rest is history. Smallpox decimated native numbers and they endured much abuse at the hands of the Spaniards until the new mixed-blood 'Raza' finally declared independence in 1810. That they won, but political turmoil between liberals and conservatives ensued and they lost Texas, then most of their northern territories to the USA. Civil unrest ensued until liberals and Benito Juarez triumphed... temporarily.

There followed a French occupation, then the long "Porfiriato" of Porfirio Diaz, which tried to mimic American success by aping them and giving them whatever they wanted. Actually the country developed much during that period, but Diaz wouldn't adapt and change, so the real civil war came in 1910. Since then until recently Mexico has had the "perfect dictatorship" of its one ruling party PRI. They expropriated the foreign oil fields and embarked on steady growth until 1982, when oil prices plunged, the currency devalued, and inflation took off running. Economic turmoil ensued until passage of the North American Free Trade Agreement in 1994. Despite that, or because of it, the economy collapsed and had to be rescued by the US. Economic reforms finally resulted and an opposition party won the presidency in 2000. Fast forward to the present...

Everybody knows about the rough patch that Mexico is going through right now, with drug cartel-related violence and all that uncertainty. What you don't hear so much about is Mexico's rapid rise from the ranks of poverty and its steady emergence as a middle–class country and economic power. In many ways it parallels that of Russia, at one and the same time a rising BRIC (Brazil, Russia India & China) economic power, and a semi-lawless mafia state with more billionaires than anywhere else in the world. Mexico is definitely in the G20 second-tier of economic power that includes Turkey, South Africa, Australia, South Korea, and others, in addition to the first-tier G8 countries. Mexico even has the richest man in the world—Carlos Slim; did you know that? It is also in tenth place for tourist arrivals in the world. That's a statistic to be proud of.

Like its northern neighbors, Mexico, too, is vast, and even more diverse, with more than fifty indigenous languages in addition to the predominant Spanish. As for the current troubles, well, it could just be one of the growing pains of democracy, not unlike the gun control issue up north or the Quebec issue in Canada. Like I've already said, you're not likely to experience it yourself. Mostly it's gang-on-gang, despite the fact that any kidnapping of an American will surely make headlines back in the US. Just be aware or your surroundings, and don't act like a stupid tourist. You should be okay, but of course (disclaimer here): *I make no guarantees for your safety, whether in Mexico, Canada, or the USA.* There, I've said it. Now let's travel. Wait a minute...

If you're an old hand in Mexico, then you could be excused for not being aware of the current hostel trend, and if you're a newbie winging it, then you may be surprised when you go into the local *hostal* and if doesn't seem like a hostel at all. We need to clarify terms again. Mexican hostels tend to use their term *hostal* somewhat interchangeably with the English loanword 'hostel' even though *hostales* long predate the current trend and therefore do not necessarily have the same meaning and connotations. In Spain they never use the word *hostal* in the name for a hostel, and in fact *albergue* may be the more correct term when used in common speech. Shared rooms certainly have some history in Latin America, though, as I distinctly remember them from Peru in 1978.

A couple of perks for Mexican hostels are that checkout times are usually noon or later, and check-in times sometimes "flexible." They frequently have swimming pools, too, at least in beach hostels. Some don't have websites, but the ones here do, and they're some of the best I've ever seen. Even better is that Mexicans are some of the friendliest people in the world. Since I traveled here first, I didn't always appreciate that, and assumed it was like that everywhere. It's not. I love Mexico. Did I mention that there are thirty-one UNESCO world heritage sites? Now let's travel.

46) Aguascalientes

AGUASCALIENTES is a city of about a million in the state of the same name, in north central Mexico, at an elevation of 6200ft/1900mt, and one of its nicer ones, neat and clean. The district of San Marcos is famous for its fair and baroque church. Guadalupe is very Spanish, with the Posada museum and eponymous church. As the name suggests, there are hot springs.

Hostal Posada, Eduardo J Correa 139, Centro Histórico, Aguascalientes, AGS; *hihostels.com/*, T:+(52)449.9186436, *aguascalientes@hostellingmexico.com*; $11Bed, Pvt.room:Y, Kitchen:Y, B'fast:Y, WiFi:Y, Locker:Y, Recep:24/7; Note: resto/bar, forex, laundry, luggage room, maps

47) Baja California

ENSENADA is a city of 280,000 — third-largest in the state — and one of the nicer ones, hugging the coast like a long-lost lover. At only ninety minutes south of the border, it's one of the more accessible ones, also. It used to be my base in North America a decade ago, before the cruise ships came in, the TJ scene moved south, and the entertainment scene became more gringo-oriented. Still it's nice, smoked marlin, oohh..

Ensenada Backpacker, Segunda 1429, Obrera, Ensenada, BC; T:+52.646.177.1758, *Info@ ensenadabackpacker.com/*; $18Bed, Pvt.room:N, Kitchen:Y, B'fast:Y, WiFi:Y, Locker:Y, Recep:24/7; Note: bikes, TV, tour desk, luggage room, parking, books, games

LORETO is a town of almost 15,000 on the interior eastern gulf side of Baja California. Founded in 1697, it was the first capital of The Californias, before it was moved to

Monterey in 1777. After that Loreto languished until targeted for tourism a couple decades ago. In addition to aquatic activities and historical missions, there are cave paintings of anthropological importance, several of UNESCO quality.

Coyote Village, Padre Kino, Loreto; *coyotevillageinc.com/*, T:+52.613.135.1933, *mikedomingue@msn.com*; $30Bed, Pvt.room:Y, Kitchen:Y, B'fast:Y, WiFi:Y, Locker:Y, Recep:ltd; Note: cash only, free drinks, pool, bikes, gym, hot tub, bar, billiards

48) Chiapas

PALENQUE is best known as the set of pre-Columbian Mayan ruins that adorn the landscape of southern Chiapas, but there is also a town here, with almost 40,000 people. The locals are mostly Ch'ol Mayan, and there is a Mayan World Festival to celebrate their culture. There are feasts of St. Dominic and St. Francis of Assissi. You can head to San Cristobal de las Casas from here, passing by the Agua Azul waterfalls, very nice...

Yaxkin Hostel, Calle 5ta Pte. Norte #2, Zona Eco-Turística La Cañada; T:+52.916.345.0102, *reservaciones@ hostalyaxkin.com/*; $9Bed, Pvt.room:Y, Kitchen:Y, B'fast:$, WiFi:Y, Locker:Y, Recep:ltd; Note: jungle theme, near ruins, resto/bar, bikes, luggage room, tour desk

SAN CRISTOBAL DE LAS CASAS (*Tzotzil*: Jovel) is a city of 150,000 sitting up in the mountains in Mexico's southernmost state of Chiapas at an altitude of 7200ft/2200mt. Culturally this area is more closely related to Guatemala, and forms part of the modern Maya triangle that stretches east to the Caribbean and north to Yucatan, and loosely paralleling a classical ruins tour of Palenque-Copan-Tikal-Chichen Itza. To this day highland Guatemalans call themselves *Chapines*, and some tribal groups are found on both sides of the border, the Mexican counterparts frequently reinvigorated by the influx of refugees from the Guatemalan wars of the 1980's.

The villages surrounding San Cristobal — Chamula, Tenejapa, Huixtán, Teopisca, Totolapa, Chiapilla, San Lucas and Zinacantán — are very traditional and some feature full costumes and crafts.

The city's historic center is very colonial and traditional — and a designated "Pueblo Magico" — at the same time that it has been heavily influenced by the influx of foreign ex-pats who have fallen in love with the place and put down roots. So that means there are reggae bars and vegan restaurants and many cultural amenities of that sort in addition to the traditional indigenous/ Spanish mix (better than go-go bars and strip clubs, right?). The traditional elements include — in addition to red-tile roofs and cobblestone streets — such events as a Feria de la Primavera y la Paz and Festival Cervantino Barroco, as well as an elaborate Holy Week celebration. There are numerous cathedrals and churches, Santo Domingo foremost of them, plus other museums and cultural centers. There is even some 'Zapatourism' based on the EZLN jungle-based uprising of a couple decades ago, and consisting of merchandise with such revolutionary themes. The countryside is mixed alpine, with pines and other, currently heavily deforested. It's cool.

Posada Del Abuelito, Tapachula 18, S.C. de las Casas, Chiapas; *hostelsancristobalchiapas.com/*, T:+52.1967.678.1741, *posadaabuelito@live.com. mx;* $9Bed, Pvt.room:Y, Kitchen:Y, B'fast:Y, WiFi:Y, Locker:N, Recep:6a>12m; Note: arpt trans, luggage rm, tour desk, laundry, tea/coffee

Iguana Hostel, Chiapa de Corzo 16, Barrio el Cerrillo, S. C. las Casas; T:+52.1967.631.7731, *Info@ iguanahostel.com/;* $7Bed, Pvt.room:Y, Kitchen:Y, B'fast:Y, WiFi:Y, Locker:Y, Recep:24/7; Note: tour desk, parking, bikes, salsa lessons, birthday parties, buses>Guat

Posada Mi Casa, Calle Ejercito Nacional 14, S.C. de las Casas; *posada-mi-casa.tripod.com/*, $8Bed, *posada-mi-casa@lycos.com;* Pvt.room:Y, Kitchen:Y, B'fast:N, WiFi:Y, Locker:N, Recep:6a>12m; Note: tea/coffee, books. Central, puppy

El Hostalito, Profa. María Adelina Flores 24, S.C. de las Casas, Chiapas; *elhostalito.wordpress.com/*, T:+52.967.631.7405, *elhostalito@hotmail.com;* $8Bed, Pvt.room:Y, Kitchen:Y, B'fast:Y, WiFi:Y, Locker:Y, Recep:ltd; Note: books, luggage room, bikes

Hostal Akumal, Av. 16 Sept. #33, (bet. Guat/Venez), S.C. de Las Casas; *hostalakumal@hotmail.com*, T:+52.967.116.1120, $10Bed, Pvt.room:Y,

Kitchen:Y   *facebook.com/pages/HostalAkumal/144708358914982;*   B'fast:Y, WiFi:Y, Locker:N, Recep:ltd; Note: arpt trans, bikes, books, maps, tea/ coffee, luggage room

Rossco Backpackers Hostel, Real de Mexicanos 16, S.C. de las Casas; T:+52(967)674.0525, *contact@ backpackershostel.com.mx/;* $8Bed, Pvt.room:Y, Kitchen:Y, B'fast:Y, WiFi:Y, Locker:Y, Recep:24/7; Note: billiards, books, forex, luggage rm, tour desk, laundry, parking

Hostal Los Camellos, Calle real de Guadalupe n°110, S.C. de las Casas; *loscamellos.over-blog.com/,* T:01(967)116.0097, *loscamellos@hotmail.com;* $8Bed, Pvt.room:Y, Kitchen:Y, B'fast:$, WiFi:Y, Locker:Y, Recep:24/7; Note: café, forex, tour desk, luggage room, tea/coffee

Puerta Vieja Hostel, Diego de Mazariegos 23, S.C. de las Casas; T:+52.967.631.4335, *contact@ puertaviejahostel.com/;* $10Bed, Pvt.room:Y, Kitchen:Y, B'fast:Y, WiFi:Y, Locker:N, Recep:ltd; Note: café, arpt trans, shuttle, tour desk, luggage room, tea/coffee

Hostal La Casa De Paco, Diego de Mazariegos #80, S.C. de las Casas: T/F:964.583.418, *david@ hostalcasapaco.com/;* $8Bed, Pvt.room:Y, Kitchen:Y, B'fast:Y, WiFi:Y, Locker:Y, Recep:ltd; Note: café/bar, bikes, parking, tea/ coffee, games

Posada Leon De Jovel, Calle Francisco Leon, #35, Santa Lucia, S.C; *Info@ leondejovel.com/,* T:+52.967.631.4535; $8Bed, Pvt.room:Y, Kitchen:Y, B'fast:N, WiFi:Y, Locker:Y, Recep:24/7; Note: wheelchair OK, tour desk, books, games, tea/cof

Coletos Hostel, Diego Dugelay 11, SC las Casas; T:+52.967.123.1122, *bookings@ coletos.com/;* $9Bed, Pvt.room:Y, Kitchen:Y, B'fast:Y, WiFi:Y, Locker:Y, Recep:24/7; Note: café, books, games, luggage room

Posada Mexico, Josefa Ortiz 12, Col. Centro Historico, SC de Las Casas; *hihostels.com/,* T:+52.967.6316912 , *mexicoposada_hostel@hotmail.com;* $13Bed, Pvt.room:Y, Kitchen:Y, B'fast:Y, WiFi:Y, Locker:Y, Recep:24/7; Note: historic house, bar, bikes, books, forex, luggage rm, tour desk, laundry

La Catrina Posada B&B, Madero 35, Esq Av. Josefa Ortiz de Dominguez, SC; T:(967)678.1067, *lacatrinaposada@gmail.com;* $Bed, Pvt.room:N, Kitchen:Y, B'fast:$, WiFi:Y, Locker:N, Recep:ltd; Note: meals, laundry

TUXTLA GUTIERREZ is a modern city of a half million in the southernmost state of Chiapas, its capital, largest city, financial center, and transportation hub. You'll likely be here to transfer buses or catch a flight. There is not much of tourist interest, but it is one of Mexico's safest cities, so maybe there's a connection. There IS a museum of anthropology, though, plus a Casa de Cultura, and a large traditional market by the zoo.

Hostal San Miguel, 3a. Avenida Sur Pte, Tuxtla Gutiérrez; *hostalsanmiguel.com.mx/*, T:961.611.4459, *hostalsanmiguel@hotmail.com*; $13Bed, Pvt.room:Y, Kitchen:Y, B'fast:$, WiFi:Y, Locker:Y, Recep:24/7; Note: central, luggage room, arpt trans, laundry, resto, c.c. OK, parking

Hostel Tres Central, Calle Central Norte 393, Tuxtla Gutierrez; *hostaltrescentral@gmail.com*; T:961.611.3674, *facebook.com/TresCentral/info*; $13Bed, Pvt.room:N, Kitchen:N, B'fast:N, WiFi:Y, Locker:Y, Recep:24/7; Note: luggage room, parking

49) Colima

COLIMA is capital of the state of the same name, and second-largest, after Manzanillo, with a population over 130,000. Being the inland capital of a coastal state is not always the best business model, and Manzanillo overshadows it as a tourist destination. Its main attraction is its lack of attractions, authentic Mexico.

El Litchi Hostal, Calle 27 de Sept. 307, Lomas Vista Hermosa, Colima; *facebook.com/ellitchi.hostalcolima/*, T:+52.131.2137.2232; $13Bed, Pvt.room:Y, Kitchen:N, B'fast:N, WiFi:N, Locker:N, Recep:24/7; Note: cash only, central, wh/chair OK, tour desk, luggage room

50) Guanajuato

GUANAJUATO is a city of 150,000 and a UNESCO world heritage site in north-central Mexico. At 6600ft/2000mt, and with narrow winding streets, it definitely has the character of a Spanish colonial mining city. La Valenciana mine produced two-thirds of the world's silver at one point. Today it produces slim fit tourists, exercising regularly. The big deal is the Festival Cervantino, a world-reknowned arts event. There is also a Mummy Museum. Apparently the locals were petrified for some reason.

Hostel Alonso, Alonso 24, Zona Centro, Guanajuato; *hostelalonso. com/*, T:+52.473.129.1131, *hostel.alonso.gto@gmail.com*; $10Bed, Pvt.room:Y, Kitchen:Y, B'fast:Y, WiFi:Y, Locker:Y, Recep:24/7; Note: café, laundry, terrace, TV, cash only

Al Son De Los Santos, De San Sebastián 94, Zona Centro, Guanajuato; *alsondelossantos.com/*, T:+52.473.7313368, *alsondelossantos@hotmail.com*; $18Bed, Pvt.room:Y, Kitchen:Y, B'fast:N, WiFi:Y, Locker:Y, Recep:ltd; Note: arpt trans, café/bar, luggage, tour desk, maps, tea/coffee

La Casa De Dante, Zaragoza 25 De La Presa, Guanajuato; *casadedante. com/*, T:+52.473.731.0909, *hospedaje_dante@hotmail.com*; $21Bed, Pvt.room:Y, Kitchen:Y, B'fast:Y, WiFi:Y, Locker:Y, Recep:24/7; Note: 165 steps, café, books, fax, tour desk, luggage rm, laundry

Hostel Casa Del Angel, Calle Posito #17, Centro Historico, Guanajuato, Gto. T:(52)473.732.3467, *hostelcasadelangel.infored.mx/*, $9Bed, Pvt.room:Y, Kitchen:Y, B'fast:Y, WiFi:Y, Locker:Y, Recep:ltd; Note: arpt trns, café, tour desk, bsic

La Casa Del Tio, Cantarranas 47, Zona Centro, Guanajuato; *lacasadeltiohostel.com/*, T:+52.473.733.9728, *lacasadeltio@hotmail.com*; $14Bed, Pvt.room:Y, Kitchen:N, B'fast:Y, WiFi:Y, Locker:Y, Recep:24/7; Note: central, resto/bar, bikes, minimart, forex, tour desk, luggage room

SAN MIGUEL DE ALLENDE is a small colonial city of over 100,000, and, perhaps more than any other in Mexico, the one that Americans discovered, saved, and proceeded to reinvent to their own specs. That means art and language schools and students, foreign retirees, an English-language library, consulate, vegan restaurants and tourists. The big attractions are the historic center and the nearby Sanctuary of Atotonilco, both UNESCO world heritage sites. Neil Casady died on the tracks outside town in 1968.

Hostel Inn, Calzada de la Luz # 31-A Centro, San Miguel de Allende, *hostelinnmx.com/*, T:+52.415.154.6727, *hostelinnmexico@yahoo.com*; $13Bed, Pvt. room:Y, Kitchen:Y, B'fast:$, WiFi:Y, Locker:Y, Recep:24/7; Note: café, tour desk, luggage rm, laundry, maps, books, terrace

Iron House Hostel, H. Colegio Militar 17, San Miguel de Allende; *iron-house-hostel.blogspot.com/*, T:+52.415.154.6108, *ihh_sma@hotmail.com*; $10Bed, Pvt.room:Y, Kitchen:Y, B'fast:$, WiFi:Y, Locker:N, Recep:24/7; Note: arpt trans, parking, luggage room, meals

Hostal Punto 79, Mesones 79, San Miguel de Allende; *reservaciones@ punto79.com/*, T:+52.415.121.1034, $16Bed, Pvt.room:Y, Kitchen:Y, B'fast:N, WiFi:Y, Locker:N, Recep:ltd; Note: billiards, tour desk

51) Guerrero

TAXCO is a city of 50,000 perched on top of a hill at 5800ft/1750meters. It is famous for its silverwork, made of silver from nearby mines. The narrow winding streets are not only picturesque but dangerous. I almost had a heart attack when I got stuck driving up and couldn't turn around until I reached the very top. It's 105mi/170km south of DF.

Hostal Joan Sebastian, Calle Joan Sebastian #20, Taxco, Gro; *hoteljoansebastian.com/*, T:01(762)622.4914, *js_taxco@yahoo.com.mx*; $10Bed, Pvt.room:Y, Kitchen:Y, B'fast:N, WiFi:Y, Locker:N, Recep:ltd; Note: laundry, parking

TRONCONES is a rustic beach village of about 600 people 20mi/32km north of Zihuatanejo. There are beaches, surfing, free-range chickens, and the Burro Boracho.

Troncones Point Surf Club & Hostel, Troncones, Guerrero; *tronconespoint. com/*, T:MEX.755.553.2886; $25Bed, Pvt.room:Y, Kitchen:Y, B'fast:$, WiFi:Y, Locker:Y, Recep:24/7; Note: eco-friendly, resto/bar, bikes, books, luggage rm, parking, tour desk

ZIHUATANEJO, aka Ixtapa-Zihuatnejo—reflecting its tourist plug-in on the edge of the 'real' town—is a municipality of 100,000 on the Pacific coast 150mi/240km north of Acapulco, the so-called 'Costa Grande.' It is also one of the more important tourist areas, also, its two halves reflecting two eras of Mexican tourism—Zihuatanejo proper going back to the 60's Acapulco era and Ixtapa reflecting the 80's era of government direction and promotion. The earlier is the more authentic, of course, if that's what you want. There is a Sail Fest in February and a Guitar Fest in March.

El Rincon Del Viajero, Paseo Las Salinas #50, Zihuatanejo; *rinconviajerozihua.4t.com/*, T:+52.755.103.4566, *rinconviajerozihua@gmail.com;*

$12Bed, Pvt.room:Y, Kitchen:Y, B'fast:Y, WiFi:Y, Locker:Y, Recep:ltd; Note: arpt trans, resto/bar, bikes, luggage rm, tour desk, laundry, parking

52) Jalisco

GUADALAJARA is a city of a million and a half in the city proper, three times that in the metro area. It is Mexico's second city in every way, and in many ways epitomizes modern Mexico much more than Mexico City, DF itself. For one thing, it is oriented toward the north and west, with little indigenous influence, and a nod to the cowboy culture that largely defines Mexico. For another it is broad and sprawling, like Mexico the country, not cramped and crowded like Mexico City. This is the birthplace of mariachi music and *charro* culture. The historic center consists of Parque Morelos, Plaza de los Mariachis, Plaza Fundadores, Plaza Tapatia, Plaza del Agave, Parque Revolucion, Jardin del Santuario, Plaza de Armas, Plaza de la Liberacion, Plaza Guadalajara and the Rotonda de los Hombres Ilustres, so no problem finding a place to sit and relax. Museums include the Regional Museum of Jalisco, Wax Museum, Trompo Mágico children's museum, Museum of Anthropology, and Hospicio Cabañas, a World Heritage Site. Enjoy.

Blue Pepper Hostel, Alfredo R. Plascencia 78. Guadalajara, Jalisco; *contact@ bluepepperhostel.com/*, T:+52.33.3615.2588; $10Bed, Pvt.room:Y, Kitchen:Y B'fast:Y, WiFi:Y Locker:Y Recep:24/7; Note: café, bikes, billiards, books, tour desk, luggage rm, parking, laundry

Hostel Tequila Backpackers, Av Hidalgo 1160 Centro, Guadalajara, Jal; *contact@ tequilahostel.com/*, T:+52.33.3146.0340; $15Bed, Pvt.room:Y, Kitchen:N, B'fast:Y, WiFi:Y, Locker:Y, Recep:24/7; Note: pool, billiards, parking, luggage room

Hostel Hospedarte Centro, Maestranza #147, Downtown, Guadalajara;

Hostel Hospedarte Chapultepec, Efraín González Luna 2075, Guadalajara; *reserve@ contacto@ hospedartehostel.com/*, T:+52.33.3615.4957; $9Bed, Pvt. room:Y, Kitchen:Y, B'fast:Y, WiFi:Y, Locker:Y, Recep:24/7; Note: billiards, bikes, books, tour desk, luggage rm, laundry, forex

Degollado Hostel, Degollado 20, Planta Alta, Guadalajara; T:+52.33.3613.6331, *Info@ degolladohostel.com/*, $13Bed, Pvt.room:Y, Kitchen:N, B'fast:Y, WiFi:Y, Locker:Y, Recep:24/7; Note: arpt trans, pool, café, bikes, tour desk, luggage rm, parking, forex

Hostel Galeria, Morelos 1281, Guadalajara; T:+52.33.3825.3801, *contacto@ hostalgaleria.com/*; $14Bed, Pvt.room:Y, Kitchen:Y, B'fast:Y, WiFi:Y, Locker:Y, Recep:24/7; Note: café/bar, arpt trans, bikes, books, tour desk, luggage rm, laundry

Lion Hostel, Miguel de Cervantes Saavedra 6, Guadalajara, Jalisco; T:+52.33.4040.5751, *Info@ lionhostel.com/*; $15Bed, Pvt.room:Y, Kitchen:Y, B'fast:Y, WiFi:Y, Locker:Y, Recep:24/7; Note: 1400 checkout! arpt trans, café, bikes, gym, hair dryers, TV, bar

Hostal D Maria, Nueva Galicia 924, Zona Centro, Guadalajara; T:+52.33.3614.6230; *reservaciones@ hostaldemaria.com/*; $14Bed, Pvt.room:Y, Kitchen:Y, B'fast:Y, WiFi:Y, Locker:Y, Recep:24/7; Note: wh/chair OK, tour desk, luggage rm, laundry, tea/coffee, maps

Hostelito Inn, Av Alcade 409, Centro Turistico, Guadalajara; *hostelitoinngdl. wix.com/*, T:(33)15.92.38.29, *Hostelitoinn@hotmail.com;* $13Bed, Pvt.room:Y, Kitchen:Y, B'fast:N, WiFi:Y, Locker:Y, Recep:24/7; Note: café, bikes, terrace

PUERTO VALLARTA is a city of a quarter million on the Pacific coast in the state of Jalisco. Once a remote village, it rose to prominence in the 60's and began attracting international tourists. Direct flights to the US began, as did rapid expansion. Workers' conditions were squalid and some beaches not swimmable because of pollution—growing pains. It is now a modern coastal city with *malecon, mercados, y museos*. We're not in Gringo Gulch anymore, Toto.

Vallarta Sun Hostel, Fca. Rodríguez 169, Emiliano Zapata, Pto Vallarta; T:+52.322.223.1529, *vallartasunhostel.com/*; $16Bed, Pvt.room:Y, Kitchen:Y, B'fast:N, WiFi:Y, Locker:Y, Recep:24/7; Note: hot tub, forex, tour desk, luggage rm, parking, laundry, books

Oasis Hostel, Libramiento 222, Col. Benito Juarez, Puerto Vallarta;

Oasis Downtown Vallarta Hostel, Juárez 386, Pto. Vallarta; T:+52.322.222.2636, *Info@ oasishostel.com/*; $15Bed, Pvt.room:Y, Kitchen:Y, B'fast:Y, WiFi:Y, Locker:Y, Recep:24/7; Note: bar, bikes, forex, tour desk, luggage rm, parking, cash only

TEQUILA is a city of 30,000 or so, famous for you-know-what. Besides distilleries, there are colonial vestiges like the main parish church, Our Lady of the Purísima Concepción, and the National Museum of Tequila. There is an annual festival every November-December. The Sanctuary of Saint Toribio Romo González is 10km away.

Hostel Viajero, Luis Navarro, Tequila, Jalisco, Mexico; T:+52.374.742.2502, *web@ hostelviajero.com/*; $10Bed, Pvt.room:Y, Kitchen:Y, B'fast:Y, WiFi:Y, Locker:N, Recep:ltd; Note: bar, tour info, cash only

53) Mexico (City), D.F.

MEXICO (CITY), D.F. is one of the world's monster cities, perched up at 7350ft/2240mt, with almost 9 million people in the city proper and God-knows-how-many in the larger metropolitan area. It was once a lake(s) basin with connected islands rising above the surface. Alas and alack, the Nahua/Mexica/Aztecs were no match for the Spaniards and their iron armor and their blunderbusses. The city gave its name to the country and is now its largest city and its capital. The *chinampas* of Xochimilco are all that's left of the original lake(s), always good for a day trip. The entire ancient city of Tenochtitlan lies thinly buried under the soils of the modern city, perhaps best viewed from the subway tunnels, since those digs are where most of it has been unearthed.

There is a huge market over at Chiconcuac, by Texcoco. Even better for authenticity is the one high up in the hills at Tianguistenco (*Nahuatl*: "marketplace"), and nearby Toluca, with goods from all over the region, including finely woven ikat *rebozos* (shawls). Otomi women pat out fresh blue corn tortillas and make squash-blossom tacos on the spot. Mexico City has numerous museums and cultural centers. Works by José Clemente Orozco, David Alfaro Siqueiros and Diego Rivera are displayed in the National Palace and the Palacio de Bellas Artes, and Frida Kahlo's house is a museum. There is also a museum of modern art. Outstanding for antiquities is the National Museum of Anthropology, unsurpassed in its collection of ancient Mexican treasures. There's nothing better than this in Cairo.

Or take a day trip out to Teotihuacan — priceless. I once talked a policeman there out of hauling my friend off to jail for climbing a pyramid, *pinche gringa*.... Strangely though, I don't think anyone considers Mexico City the heart of the country. I know I don't. I think of it more like the New York City of Mexico, that exotic erotic distillation of all that is unique and powerful about the country crammed into one small corner, so that all the rest of the country can stare at it in awe and wonder, mixed with occasional disgust. Twice I was there on the occasion of the worst pollution ever recorded, a sliding scale of abuse. They found a mutated rat a yard/meter long. Wear protection. There's nothing like it. All roads in Mexico lead here. Airport is on the subway line.

Hostel Amigo, Isabel la Catolica #61 col. Zona centro, Mex; T:+52.55.5512.3464

Hostel Amigo Suites Downtown, Luis González Obregón 14 Centro, Cuauhtémoc, T:+52.55.5510.0925, *Info@ hostelamigo.com/*; $9Bed, Pvt.room:Y, Kitchen:Y, B'fast:Y, WiFi:Y, Locker:Y, Recep:24/7; Note: bar, free arpt pickup, laundry, tours, near Zocalo

Hostel Suites DF, Terán 38 Cuauhtémoc, Col. Tabacalera, Mex DF; *hihostels.com/*, T:+52.55.5535.8117, *hostelsuitesdf@hostellingmexico.com*; $15Bed, Pvt.room:Y, Kitchen:Y, B'fast:Y, WiFi:Y, Locker:Y, Recep:8a>10p; Note: café/bar, tour desk, luggage rm, laundry, TV, c.c. OK

Hostel Cathedral, Rep. de Guatemala 4, Centro, Cuauhtémoc, Mex DF; T:+52.55.5518.1726, *Info@ mundojovenhostels.com/*; $9Bed, Pvt.room:Y, Kitchen:Y, B'fast:Y, WiFi:Y, Locker:Y, Recep:24/7; Note: resto/bar, lift, tour desk, luggage rm, laundry, books, terrace, tea/cof

Erio Hostal La Buena Vida, Mazatlan 190, Hipódromo Condesa, Cuauhtémoc; T:+52.55.5271.9799, *reservaciones@ hostallabuenavida.com/*; $20Bed, Pvt.room:N, Kitchen:Y, B'fast:Y, WiFi:Y, Locker:N, Recep:ltd; Note: resto/bar, laundry, luggage rm

Hostel Centro Historico Regina, 5 de Febrero 53, Centro, Cuauhtémoc; T:+52.55.5709.4192, *hostalcentrohistoricoregina.com/*; $9Bed, Pvt.room:Y, Kitchen:Y, B'fast:Y, WiFi:Y, Locker:Y, Recep:24/7; Note: resto/bar, forex, bikes, luggage room, tour desk, rooftop terrace

Hostel Downtown Beds, Isabel la Católica 30, Col. Centro, Mexico DF; *hihostels.com/*, T:+5255.5130.6855, *downtownbeds@hostellingmexico.com*; $17Bed, Pvt.room:Y, Kitchen:Y, B'fast:Y, WiFi:Y, Locker:Y, Recep:24/7; Note: arpt trans, bar, bikes, pool, luggage room, tour desk, laundry, forex

Mexico City Suites, Rep de Brasil 11, Cuauhtémoc; T:(0155)5510.9562

Mexico City Hostel, Rep de Brasil 8, Cuauhtémoc; T:+52.55.5512.3666, *reservaciones@ reservaciones-suites@ contact@ mexicocityhostel.com/*; $14Bed, Pvt.room:Y, Kitchen:Y, B'fast:Y, WiFi:Y, Locker:Y, Recep:24/7; Note: arpt trans, luggage room, tour desk, laundry, books, games

Massiosare El Hostel, Revillagigedo 47 PH-1, Colonia Centro, Mex DF; *massiosarehostal.com/*, T:+52.55.5521.3256, *massiosarehostal@gmail.com*; $9Bed,

Pvt.room:Y, Kitchen:Y, B'fast:Y, WiFi:Y, Locker:Y, Recep:ltd; Note: cafe, luggage room, tea/coffee, cash only, 4th floor no lift

Hostal Cuija Coyoacan, Berlin 279, Colonia del Carmen, Mexico DF; T:+52.55.5659.9310, *hostalcuijacoyoacan.com/*; $18Bed, Pvt.room:Y, Kitchen:N, B'fast:Y, WiFi:Y, Locker:Y, Recep:ltd; Note: arpt trans, parking, luggage room, not central, rooftop chill-out

Hostel333, Colima #333 Colonia Roma, Del. Cuauhtemoc, Mex DF, *reservations@ hostel333.com/*, T:+52(55)5533.3609, *hostal333@gmail.com*; $10Bed, Pvt.room:Y, Kitchen:Y, B'fast:Y, WiFi:Y, Locker:Y, Recep:24/7; Note: bar, books, laundry, luggage room, tea/coffee, terrace

Stayinn Barefoot Condesa, Eje 2 Sur (Juan Escutia) 125, Col. Condesa, Cuauhtémoc; *stayinnbarefoot.com/*, T:+52.55.6286.3000, *mexicocity@barefoot.mx*; $15Bed, Pvt.room:Y, Kitchen:Y, B'fast:Y, WiFi:Y, Locker:Y, Recep:24/7; Note: resto/bar, lift, luggage room, tour desk, laundry, parking, arpt. trans

Hostel Airport Mexico DF, Venustiano Carranza, Iztacalco, Mexico, DF; *hostelmexicodf.com/*, T:+52.55.1560.3288, *hostelmexicodf@gmail.com*; $15Bed, Pvt.room:Y, Kitchen:N, B'fast:Y, WiFi:Y, Locker:N, Recep:ltd; Note: laundry, close to intl arpt, shuttle

Hostal Boutique La Tercia, Genova #75 & #79, Mexico City, DF: *Info@ hostalboutiquelatercia.com.mx/*, T:+52.55.5533.7848; $14Bed, Pvt.room:Y, Kitchen:N, B'fast:$, WiFi:Y, Locker:Y, Recep:24/7; Note: resto, lift, luggage room, terrace

Hostal Casa Vieja, Cerrada de Londres # 7, Col. Juárez, Del. Cuauhtemoc; T:+52.55.5208.3004, *Info@ hostalcasavieja.com.mx/*; $9Bed, Pvt.room:Y, Kitchen:Y, B'fast:Y, WiFi:Y, Locker:Y, Recep:24/7; Note: 'zona Rosa', café, luggage room, tour desk, parking, near metro

Hostal Victoria DF, Cerrada de Varsovia 11, Juárez, Cuauhtémoc, Mex DF: T:+52.55.5207.1923, *hostalvictoriamexico.com/*; $9Bed, Pvt.room:Y, Kitchen:Y, B'fast:$, WiFi:Y, Locker:N, Recep:24/7; Note: cash only, café, laundry, luggage room, tea/coffee, basic

Hostel Home, Tabasco 303, Roma Norte, Cuauhtémoc, Mexico DF: T:+52.55.5511.1683, *reservaciones@ hostelhome.com.mx/*; $10Bed, Pvt.room:Y, Kitchen:Y, B'fast:Y, WiFi:Y, Locker:N, Recep:24/7; Note: café, tour desk, luggage room, forex, near supermkt

YWCA Centro Historico, Humboldt #62, Mexico City, DF: T:5510.3870, *info@ ywca.com.mx/*; $12Bed, Pvt.room:Y, Kitchen:Y, B'fast:$, WiFi:N, Locker:Y, Recep:24/7; Note: resto, gym, TV, biz center

Hostel Privanza, Etla #20, Col. Hipodromo Condesa; T:+52.55.52111024

Hostel Condesa Chapultepec, Cozumel #53-A, Col. Roma Norte, Mex DF; *hostelcondesachapultepec.com/*, $13Bed, *hi.condesa-chapultepec@hotmail.com*; Pvt.room:Y, Kitchen:N, B'fast:Y, WiFi:Y, Locker:Y, Recep:24/7; Note: tour desk, laundry, luggage room, arpt trans $, games, nice house/area

El Cenote Azul, C/Alfonso Pruneda #24, Col. Copilco El Alto, Coyoacan, DF; T:+52.55.5554.8730, *avisos@ elcenoteazul.com/*, $12Bed, Pvt.room:N, Kitchen:N, B'fast:$, WiFi:Y, Locker:Y, Recep:ltd; Note: resto/bar, luggage room, organic coffee, music

Casa Roa, Fernando Gonzalez Roa 8, Cd. Satelite, Naucalpan, Mex DF; *casa-roa.com/*, T:+52.55.5562.3445, *acasaroa@gmail.com*; $28Bed, Pvt.room:Y, Kitchen:Y, B'fast:$, WiFi:Y, Locker:Y, Recep:24/7; Note: café, hot tub, tour desk, laundry, parking, forex

54) Michoacan

MORELIA is another splendid north-central Mexican colonial gem... and UNESCO world heritage site. It is also a city of over 700,000 at an elevation of 6300ft/1900meters.

The central foci of the city are the Plaza de Armas and Cathedral of Michocan, built of pink cantera stone and featuring two sixty-meter high towers. There is a House of Culture, numerous museums, and festivals of music and film.

Hostel Tequila Sunset, Santiago Tapia #679, Col. Centro, Morelia; *hihostels.com/*, T:+52(443)313.8497, *tequilasunsethostal@gmail.com*; $15Bed, Pvt.

room:Y, Kitchen:Y, B'fast:Y, WiFi:Y, Locker:Y, Recep:24/7; Note: arpt trans, forex, tour desk, luggage room, parking

Hostal Mintzi, La Corregidora 503, Morelia; *hostalmintzi.com/*, T:+52.443.274.0631, *hostalmintzi@gmail.com;* $13Bed, Pvt.room:Y, Kitchen:Y, B'fast:Y, WiFi:Y, Locker:Y, Recep:ltd; Note: historic downtown, arpt trans, wh/chair OK, tour desk, safe dep

Hostal San Fransiskuni, Antonio Alzate 302 Col. Centro, Morelia; *hostalsanfransiskuni.com/*, T:01(443)313.0703, *hostalsanfransiskuni@hotmail.com;* $13Bed, Pvt.room:Y, Kitchen:Y, B'fast:Y, WiFi:Y, Locker:$, Recep:ltd; Note: books, tour desk, terrace, laundry, TV

Hostel Allende, Allende 843, Centro, Morelia; *hostelallende.com/*, T:+52.443.312.2246, *hostelallende@gmail.com;* $15Bed, Pvt.room:Y, Kitchen:N, B'fast:Y, WiFi:Y, Locker:Y, Recep:24/7; Note: wh/chair OK, luggage room, tour desk, c.c. OK

55) Morelos

CUERNVACA is a city of 350,000, whose reputation precedes it as "city of eternal spring." That's what the Aztec emperors thought up in Tenochtitlan, making it their summer capital. So did Bugsy Siegel, Malcolm Lowry ("Under the Volcano"), Timothy Leary, and thousands of foreign Spanish-immersion students. There are Aztec ruins and colonial landmarks. The *zocalo* is lively. There are gardens, markets, and cathedrals.

Posada Morelos, Clavijero 26, Centro, Cuernavaca; *posadamorelos.com/*, T:+52.777.119.4668, *hostelposadamorelos@hotmail.com:* $13Bed, Pvt.room:Y, Kitchen:N, B'fast:N, WiFi:Y, Locker:Y, Recep:ltd; Note: pool, tour desk, TV, downtown

56) Nayarit

SAYULITA is a town of 4000 on the Pacific coast of Nayarit, discovered not long ago by surfers and now one of the hot spots for Mexican adventure/ budget travel. It is only 25mi/40km north of Puerto Vallarta along the way to San Blas. Cora and Huichol Indians sell crafts in town. There are ample outdoor activities besides surfing, too.

Hostel San Pancho, Av. Tercer Mundo #12, San Pancho, Sayulita; *Luis@ hostelsanpancho.com/*, T:(045)311.258.4261; $12Bed, Pvt.room:Y, Kitchen:N, B'fast:$, WiFi:Y, Locker:N, Recep:24/7; Note: resto/bar, bike, arpt trans, forex, tour desk, parking, safe dep

AmazingHostelSayulita,102PelicanosSt,Sayulita;*theamazinghostelsayulita. com/*, T:+52(329)291.3688, *amazinghostel@usa.net*; $16Bed, Pvt.room:Y, Kitchen:Y, B'fast:N, WiFi:Y, Locker:Y, Recep:24/7; Note: pool, bikes, books, luggage rm, parking, laundry, tour desk, forex

57) Nuevo Leon

MONTERREY is Mexico's third-largest city, with over a million people in the city proper, and four times that in the metro area. It is generally considered the most 'American,' too, with many corporate offices and fully developed. Unfortunately these days it is also one of the most dangerous, with frequent car-jackings and other crimes of violence as part of the current wave of drug cartel wars. Be careful. Saltillo is very near.

La Casa Del Barrio, Diego de Montemayor 1221, Col Centro Barrio Antiguo; T:+52.81.8344.1800, *reservaciones@ lacasadelbarrio.com.mx/*, $14Bed,

Pvt.room:Y, Kitchen:Y, B'fast:Y, WiFi:Y, Locker:Y, Recep:24/7; Note: tour desk, laundry, old town

58) Oaxaca

MAZUNTE is a small village of less than a thousand along the southern Oaxaca coast. It grew up along with the rise in sea turtle and egg consumption, and declined when they did. Now they promote them — and eco-tourism, and eco-products — rather than hunt them... brilliant! Besides eco-tourism, there are beaches, and a music festival. *Chevere.*

Hostal El Nagual, Andador La Barrita, Mazunte, Oax; *hostalelnagual. com/*, T:+52.958.585.6133; $10Bed, Pvt.room:Y, Kitchen:Y, B'fast:N, WiFi:Y, Locker:N, Recep:24/7; Note: free arpt trans, tea/coffee, tour desk, forex

OAXACA is a pleasant city of a quarter million at an elevation of 5100ft/1550mt in the southern state of the same name. This is Mexico at its finest, where the colonial north meets the indigenous south, in this case the local Zapotecs. The surrounding villages specialize in their own handmade crafts, handwoven and embroidered textiles being among the best. Outside the valley proper are tribal mixtecs, zoques, triques, mazatecs, chinantecs, chatinos, mixe and nahuas (nahuatl-speakers, mexica, 'aztec'). The hilltop ruins of Monte Alban are nearby. There are many cathedrals and churches important historically and architecturally, along with museums and cultural centers. The Guelaguetza is the huge annual celebration, held in July. The *Noche de Rabanos* (Night of Radishes) features carved radishes on December 23. The film fest is in November. *Mole* is the regional dish par excellence. The 'ices' in the market are to die for (and I don't usually talk like that). Oaxaca is my old stomping grounds.

Cielo Rojo Hostel, Xicotencatl 121, Centro, Oax; *Info@ cielorojohostel.com/,* T:+52(951)514.1768; $11Bed, Pvt.room:Y, Kitchen:Y, B'fast:Y, WiFi:Y, Locker:Y, Recep:24/7; Note: nr bus/center, café, billiards, books, luggage rm, tour desk, laundry

Casa De Don Pablo Hostel, Melchor Ocampo 412, Centro, Oax; *casadedonpablo.com.mx/,* +52.951.516.8384, *lacasadedonpablo@yahoo.com.mx/*; $11Bed, Pvt.room:Y, Kitchen:Y, B'fast:Y, WiFi:Y, Locker:Y, Recep:24/7; Note: central, arpt trans, bar, tour desk, luggage room, c.c.OK, fax

Casa Angel Youth Hostel, Tinoco y Palacios 610, Centro. Oax; *casaangelhostel.com/,* T:+52.951.514.2224, *casaangelhostel@hotmail.com*; $11Bed, Pvt.room:Y, Kitchen:Y, B'fast:Y, WiFi:Y, Locker:Y, Recep:24/7; Note: tour desk

Hostal Luz De Luna Nuyoo, Juárez 101, Z. Centro, Oax; *hosteluzdeluna@ gmail.com*; T:+52.951.615.9576, (see FB page); $9Bed, Pvt.room:Y, Kitchen:Y, B'fast:$, WiFi:Y, Locker:Y, Recep:ltd; Note: café/bar, tea/coffee, games, maps

Azul Cielo Hostel, Arteaga Num: 608 Centro, Oax; *azulcielohostel.mex.tl/,* T:01.951.205.3564; $Bed, Pvt.room:Y, Kitchen:Y, B'fast:Y, WiFi:Y, Locker:Y, Recep:ltd; Note: central, arpt trans, bikes, tour desk, laundry, games

Hostel Don Nino, José María Pino Suárez 804, Centro, Oax; T:+52.951.502.5336, *hosteldonnino.com/;* $12Bed, Pvt.room:Y, Kitchen:Y, B'fast:Y, WiFi:Y, Locker:Y, Recep:24/7; Note: nr bus/ctr, arpt trans, resto/bar, forex, tea/coffee, luggage rm, laundry

Hostal Casa Del Sol, La Constitución 301, Centro, Oax; T:+52.951.514.4110, *reservas@ hostalcasadelsol.com.mx/;* $13Bed, Pvt.room:N, Kitchen:N, B'fast:Y, WiFi:Y, Locker:N, Recep:8a>10p; Note: books, no TV, bikes, tour desk

Hostal Don Miguel, Avenida Hidalgo #507-B, Oax; *hosteldonmiguel@ hotmail.com,* T:+52(951)516.1615, (see FB page); $9Bed, Pvt.room:Y, Kitchen:N, B'fast:N, WiFi:Y, Locker:N, Recep:24/7; Note: pool, travel desk, luggage room, cash only, basic

La Villada Inn Hostel, Felipe Angeles 204, Ejido Guadalupe Victoria, Oax; *lavillada.com/,* T:+52.951.518.6217, *lavilladainnhotel@hotmail.com*; $13Bed, Pvt.room:Y, Kitchen:N, B'fast:$, WiFi:Y, Locker:N, Recep:8a>10p; Note: far north of city, resto/bar/club, pool, billiards, books, forex, parking

Plaza Del Carmen Hostel, Mariano Matamoros 305, Centro, Oax; *plazadelcarmen.net/,* T:+52.951.514.5877, *pdcoaxaca@gmail.com*; $17Bed, Pvt.

room:Y, Kitchen:N, B'fast:$, WiFi:Y, Locker:Y, Recep:ltd; Note: resto/bar, wh/ chair OK, tour desk, luggage room, tea/coffee, basic

Paulina Youth Hostel, Trujano 321, col. Centro, Oax; T:09515162005, *reservations@ paulinahostel.com/*; $16Bed, Pvt.room:N, Kitchen:Y, B'fast:Y, WiFi:Y, Locker:Y, Recep:24/7; Note: luggage rm, tour desk, laundry, parking, TV, central

Nizadú Hostel, 5a Privada de la Noria 316. Colonia Centro, Oax; *facebook. com/nizadu/info*, T:+52.951.514.0707, *welcome@nizaduhostel.com*; $13Bed, Pvt. room:Y, Kitchen:Y, B'fast:Y, WiFi:Y, Locker:Y, Recep:24/7; Note: arpt trns, bar, bikes, forex, luggage rm, tour desk, parking,

PUERTO ESCONDIDO is a city of 25,000 on the southern Oaxacan coast, seven hours (it used to be twelve) by road over the hills from the capital, also accessible by bus from either direction along the coast. The beach is nice, surf is good, and so is the seafood. This was my first destination as a solo international traveler back in 1976. Smoothies were a quarter, and the Frito Bandido held us up on the beach. It's changed.

Hostal Losodeli, Prol. 2a Norte s/n, esq, Cta. Costera 405, Pto Escondido; T:(954)582.42.21, *losodeli@ hostelpuertoescondido.com/*; $9Bed, Pvt.room:Y, Kitchen:Y, B'fast:N, WiFi:Y, Locker:Y, Recep:ltd; Note: pool, bar, tour desk, luggage room, parking, Puerto Angelito

Hotel & Youth Hostal Mayflower, Andador Libertad, Pto Escondido; *tomzap.com/mayflower.html/*, T:(954)582.0367, *minnemay@hotmail.com*; $11Bed, Pvt.room:Y, Kitchen:Y, B'fast:N, WiFi:Y, Locker:Y, Recep:24/7; Note: billiards, forex, tour desk, luggage room, parking, ½ blk>beach,

Osa Mariposa, Priv. de Cancun s/n, Colonia Brisas De Zicatela, Pto Escondido; *Info@ osamariposa.com/*, T:(521)954.110.8354; $8Bed, Pvt.room:Y, Kitchen:N, B'fast:$, WiFi:Y, Locker:N, Recep:24/7; Note: resto/bar, forex, tour desk, luggage rm, parking, games, bikes, far

Cabo Blanco Hostel, #7 Playa Zicatela, Brisas de Zicatela, Oaxaca; *caboblanco.hostel.com/*, T:+52.954.582.0337, *caboblancosloid8.blogspot.com/*; $6Bed, Pvt.room:Y, Kitchen:Y, B'fast:$, WiFi:Y, Locker:Y, Recep:ltd; Note: resto/bar/club, billiards, parking, terrace

59) Puebla

PUEBLA is yet another Mexican colonial gem and UNESCO world heritage site, housing 1.5 million people (2.5M in the metro area). At the center of it all are the *zocalo* and the surrounding buildings — City Hall, Casa de los Munecos, and Cathedral. There are countless museums and landmarks. *Mole poblano* is its most famous dish. It is also famous for its *talavera* pottery.

Hostal Santo Domingo, 4 Poniente 312, Puebla; *hihostels.com/*, T:+52.222.232.1671, *hostalstodomingo@yahoo.com.mx*; $13Bed, Pvt.room:Y, Kitchen:Y, B'fast:Y, WiFi:Y, Locker:Y, Recep:24/7; Note: café/bar, tour desk, luggage room, TV

60) Queretaro

QUERETARO is another north-central Mexican colonial gem — UNESCO quality — and a modern booming city of 800,000 where many corporations have their headquarters. Otomis were the original inhabitants, and managed to coexist with the Spaniards more peacefully then elsewhere. Except for the historic aqueduct, most historic sights are found in the old center, including the Plaza de Armas, the Church of San Francisco, and other Baroque classics. The center is pedestrian-friendly and filled with museums. The Festival de Santiago de Queretaro is an eight-day arts extravaganza during Holy Week. Nearby Sierra Gorda de Querétaro was declared by UNESCO as a Biosphere Reserve.

Kuku Ruku Green Boutique Hostels, Vergara 12, Centro, Queretaro; *Info@ kukuruku.mx/*, T:+52(442)245.8777; $13Bed, Pvt.room:Y, Kitchen:N,

B'fast:$, WiFi:Y, Locker:Y, Recep:24/7; Note: resto/bar, laundry, luggage room, a/c

Casa San Gallito Hostel, Hidalgo 47, Querétaro; T:+52.442.224.3230, *Info@ sangallito.com.mx/*; $13Bed, Pvt.room:Y, Kitchen:Y, B'fast:Y, WiFi:Y, Locker:Y, Recep:24/7; Note: café, minimart, luggage room, tour desk, terrace, historic house

Ocote Hostal, Pino Suarez 57, Queretaro; *ocotehostal.com/*, T:01(442)713.1617, *ocotehostal@gmail.com*; $11Bed, Pvt.room:Y, Kitchen:Y, B'fast:Y, WiFi:Y, Locker:Y, Recep:24/7; Note: café, tour desk, laundry, cash only, books

Itza Hostal, Francisco Fagoaga 17, Santiago de Querétaro; *itzahostal.com/ itza.html*, T:+52.442.212.4223, *reservaciones@itzahostal.com/*; $10Bed, Pvt.room:Y, Kitchen:Y, B'fast:Y, WiFi:Y, Locker:Y, Recep:24/7; Note: gym, laundry, c.c. OK

Hostal Galerie Queretaro, Ezequiel Montes Sur # 41, Centro Historico, Qto; T:+52.442.212.8055, *hostalgalerie.com/*; $12Bed, Pvt.room:Y, Kitchen:Y, B'fast:Y, WiFi:Y, Locker:Y, Recep:24/7; Note: café, minimart, luggage rm, parking, laundry, tea/coffee

61) Quintana Roo

BACALAR is a city of 11,000 in southernmost Quintana Roo, 25mi/40km north of Chetumal. Before the Spanish came in 1543, it was a Mayan city. The Fortress of San Felipe Bacalar was built in 1729 to fend off pirates, and is a landmark today. As it is on the Caribean Sea, the water is sublime, of course.

Magic Bacalar, Bet. 5th Ave/3rd Ave, St 36, Bacalar, QR; *Info@ magicbacalar. com/*; $12Bed, Pvt.room:Y, Kitchen:Y, B'fast:N, WiFi:N, Locker:N, Recep:ltd; Note: no c.c, no I-net, lagoon, camping, tours, luggage room, meals, mkt

CANCUN is a purpose-built tourist resort of 600,000 which was developed with government backing in the 1970's. I can remember when there was nothing here, nothing at all. Now it's pretty much like 'tourist zones' everywhere — beach-oriented commercial strands filled with hotels, restaurants, bars, and boutiques. It used to be known for its virgin white-sand beaches. They aren't so virgin anymore. There are Mayan ruins.

Haina Hostal, Orquideas 13 Sm.22, Cancun, QR; T:+52.998.898.2081, *Info@ hainahostal.com/*; $11Bed, Pvt.room:Y, Kitchen:Y, B'fast:Y, WiFi:Y, Locker:Y, Recep:24/7; Note: luggage room, tour desk, central, nr bus, quiet

Hostel Mundo Joven Cancún, Uxmal #25, (2blks<ADO bus), Cancún, QR; *hihostels.com/*, T:+52(998)898.2103, *a.valdez@mundojoven.com*; $13Bed, Pvt. room:Y, Kitchen:N, B'fast:Y, WiFi:Y, Locker:Y, Recep:24/7; Note: central, roof terrace, luggage room, parking, tour desk

Hostal Balam, 50 Calle Alcatraces, SM 022 M. 11, Cancun, QR; *desk@ hostalbalam.com/*, T:+52(998)884.0397; $10Bed, Pvt.room:Y, Kitchen:?, B'fast:Y, WiFi:Y, Locker:N, Recep:24/7; Note: tea/cof, arpt trans, wh/chair OK, luggage room, hard find, tour desk

Hostel Ka'beh Cancun, Alcatraces 45 SM. 22 Mza 10 L.26, Retorno 5, Cancun; T:+52.998.892.7902, *hostelkabeh@gmail.com*, (see FB page); $8Bed, Pvt.room:N, Kitchen:Y, B'fast:Y, WiFi:Y, Locker:Y, Recep:24/7; Note: café, wh/chair OK, luggage room, parking, tour desk, forex, minimart

Hostel Quetzal, Orquideas N° 10, Cancun, QR; *contact@ quetzal-hostel.com/*, T:01.998.883.9821; $13Bed, Pvt.room:Y, Kitchen:N, B'fast:Y, WiFi:Y, Locker:Y, Recep:24/7; Note: free meals, resident DJ, café/bar, pool, gym, arpt trans, PARTY!!!zzz

Hostel Meson De Tulum, Av Tulum 21, Cancún, QR; T:+52.998.898.3142, *reservaciones@ mesontulum.com/*; $9Bed, Pvt.room:Y, Kitchen:N, B'fast:Y, WiFi:Y, Locker:N, Recep:24/7; Note: pool, café, luggage room, parking, tour desk, a/c, central, nr bus

Bed & Breakfast Garden, Jicama 7, Cancún, QR; T:+52.998.267.7777, *bedandbreakfastcancun.com.mx/*, $13Bed, Pvt.room:Y, Kitchen:Y, B'fast:Y, WiFi:Y, Locker:N, Recep:ltd; Note: yoga, surf, café, tea/coffee, parking, games

Hotel Soberanis, Av. Coba 5 y 7. Manzana 8 SM 22, Cancun, QR; T:+52.998.884.1540, *reservas@ hotelsoberanis.com/*; $10Bed, Pvt.room:Y,

Kitchen:N, B'fast:Y, WiFi:Y, Locker:Y, Recep:24/7; Note: 4bed dorm = room w/2dbl, resto/bar, wh/chair OK, forex, luggage rm

Hotel Sotavento, 4Km Bul. Kukulcan, calle del pescador lote d, Cancun; *sotavento@ hotelsoberanis.com/*, T:+52.998.849.4707; $18Bed, Pvt.room:Y, Kitchen:N, B'fast:Y, WiFi:Y, Locker:N, Recep:24/7; Note: yacht club/hotel, resto/bar, pool, wh/chair OK, forex, tour desk, biz ctr

Moloch Hostel, Margaritas 54, Cancún, QR; *hihostels.com/*, T:+52.998.884.6918, *molochhostel@yahoo.com.mx;* $15Bed, Pvt.room:N, Kitchen:Y, B'fast:Y, WiFi:Y, Locker:Y, Recep:24/7; Note: café, pool, minimart, luggage room, parking, tour desk, c.c.

Hostal Marpez, Crisantemos 20, S.M.22, Cancun, QR: *reservaciones@ hostalmarpez.com.mx/*, T:+52.998.892.4789; $10Bed, Pvt.room:Y, Kitchen:Y, B'fast:Y, WiFi:Y, Locker:N, Recep:24/7; Note: central, parking, basic

Hostal Mayapan, Boulevard Kukulkan 5, Cancún, QR; T:+52.998.883.3227, *Info@ hostalmayapan.com/*; $18Bed, Pvt.room:Y, Kitchen:N, B'fast:Y, WiFi:Y, Locker:?, Recep:24/7; Note: hotel zone, minimart, luggage rm, a/c

CHETUMAL is a city of 150,000 on the border of Mexico with Belize. As such it is not so much a tourist town as a commercial and governmental one. This was a major front in the 1848 Caste War waged by Mayan Indians against whites and mestizos, sending many refugees across the border into (then) British Honduras. Things are calmer now.

La Posada Chetumal, Av Venustiano Carranza 481, Col. Flamboyanes; *laposadachetumalhostel.com.mx/*, $14Bed, Pvt.room:Y, Kitchen:Y, B'fast:Y, WiFi:Y, Locker:Y, Recep:24/7; Note: hot tub, meals, wh/chair, luggage rm, parking, laundry, cash only, far

COZUMEL is an island in the Mexican Caribbean with a population of 100,000, and at one time the premier destination for budget travel in the area. Now that it is dwarfed by the tourist zoos of Cancun and Playas del Carmen, its reputation is only enhanced for me. There are Mayan ruins here. Apparently it was a place of pilgrimage for its fertility-enhancing properties. Sun, sand, and warm breezes will do that to you... Diving's good.

Hostelito, 10a Av. Norte 42, Centro, Cozumel, QR; *hostelcozumel.com/*, T:+52.987.869.8157, *hostelitocozumelmex@gmail.com*; $12Bed, Pvt.room:Y, Kitchen:Y, B'fast:N, WiFi:Y, Locker:Y, Recep:ltd; Note: bikes, tour desk, luggage room, a/c, nr beach

Amigos Hostel Cozumel, C. 7 Sur # 571 bet. Ave 25&30 col. Centro Cozumel; *cozumelhostel.com/*, T:+52.987.872.3868, *cozumelhostel@gmail.com*; $12Bed, Pvt. room:Y, Kitchen:Y, B'fast:$, WiFi:Y, Locker:Y, Recep:ltd; Note: café, pool, tea/ coffee, tour desk, luggage room, parking, billiards

HOLBOX ISLAND lies off the northern coast of the Yucatan peninsula in the state of Quintana Roo. Still in the early phase of tourism, there are not much more than 1200 folks, and few if any cars. Fishing and whale-shark viewing are popular, but kite-boarding is the big deal. Access is by ferry from Chiquila.

Tribu Hostel, Av. Pedro Joaquin Coldwell, Mz.19 Lt 6, Isla Holbox, QR; T:+52.984.875.2507, *Info@ tribuhostel.com*; $10Bed, Pvt.room:Y, Kitchen:Y, B'fast:N, WiFi:Y, Locker:Y, Recep:ltd; Note: bar, bikes, books, forex, luggage room, tour desk: kites/kayaks/fish

Hostel Ida Y Vuelta, Calle P. E. Calles s/n, Entre Robalo y Chacchi, Isla Holbox; *holboxhostel.blogspot.com/*, T:+52.984.875.2358, *idayvueltacamping@ yahoo.com*; $8Bed, Pvt.room:Y, Kitchen:Y, B'fast:Y, WiFi:Y, Locker:N, Recep:24/7; Note: arpt trans, resto/bar, bikes, tour desk, luggage rm, laundry, parking

ISLA MUJERES is an island town of 12-13,000 off the northern Yucatan peninsula in the Caribbean-facing state of Quintana Roo. Apparently a Mayan fertility pilgrimage site, like Cozumel, its name comes from the many goddess figurines found here. The coral reef is good for scuba and snorkeling. You can also swim with dolphins. There is a ferry to Puerto Juarez on the coast. I was here in 1984. My taxi driver got me stoned, while my partner freaked out, especially when we passed the military base. *Chevere.*

Poc Na Hostel, Matamoros 15, esq. Carlos Lazo, Isla Mujeres, QR; T:+52.998.877.0090, *info@ pocna.com/*; $13Bed, Pvt.room:N, Kitchen:Y, B'fast:Y, WiFi:Y, Locker:Y, Recep:ltd; Note: camping, resto/bar, bikes, billiards, books, tour desk, luggage room

PLAYA DEL CARMEN was once known as a fishing village and the terminal point for the ferry to Cancun. Now it is the primary destination in and of itself, threatening to overtake even Cancun. Despite efforts to the contrary, it is tourism of the most inauthentic type: name brands, luxury hotels and chain restaurants. Is this the new paradigm for cruise ships and/or foreign based outlet stores? We'll see. If that's what you want, then this is the place.

Green Monkey Hostel, 1st Av esq Calle 22 norte, Playa del Carmen, QR; *greenmonkeyhostel@gmail.com*; T:+52.984.876.8857, (see FB page); $15Bed, Pvt. room:Y, Kitchen:N, B'fast:Y, WiFi:Y, Locker:Y, Recep:24/7: Note: luggage room, tour desk, parking, near beach, tranquilo, a/c

Hostel Rio Playa, Calle 8 Entre 5 y ave 10, Playa del Carmen, QR; T:+52.984.803.0145, *hostelrios@gmail.com*, (see Facebook page); $13Bed, Pvt. room:Y, Kitchen:N, B'fast:Y, WiFi:Y, Locker:Y, Recep:24/7; Note: café/bar, pool, minimart, tea/coffee, forex, luggage rm, party, nr bus

Hostel Vive La Vida, Calle 2, Col Centro Playa del Carmen, QR; *hostalvivelavida.com/*, T:+52(984)109.2457, *hostalvivelavida@gmail.com*; $9Bed, Pvt.room:Y, Kitchen:Y, B'fast:N, WiFi:Y, Locker:Y, Recep:ltd; Note: pool, café, wh/chair OK, bikes, luggage rm, tour desk, laundry

Bed & Breakfast Popol Vuh, 2 Nte S/N, Centro, Playa del Carmen, QR; T:+52.984.803.2149, *bookings@ popolvuhplaya.com/*; $11Bed, Pvt.room:Y, Kitchen:Y, B'fast:Y, WiFi:Y, Locker:N, Recep:ltd; Note: on beach, resto/bar, tour desk

Hostel Che, Calle 6, entre Ave 15 & Ave 20, Playa del Carmen, QR; T:+52(984)174.1741, *Info@ hostelche.com.mx/*; $13Bed, Pvt.room:Y, Kitchen:Y, B'fast:Y, WiFi:Y, Locker:Y, Recep:24/7; Note: roof bar, resto, minimart, bikes, luggage rm, tour desk, forex, party

Grand Hostal Playa, Av 20 Entre Calles 4 y 6, Playa del Carmen, QR; T:+52(984)106.5737, *Info@ grandhostal.com/*; $12Bed, Pvt.room:Y, Kitchen:Y, B'fast:$, WiFi:Y, Locker:Y, Recep:ltd; Note: pool, café, bikes, books, luggage rm, tour desk, laundry, parking

Hotel Colorado P. Del C, Calle 4 Nte, 20>25 Av, Centro, Solidaridad, QR; T:+52.984.873.0381, *contacto@ coloradoplaya.com/*; $14Bed, Pvt.room:Y, Kitchen:Y, B'fast:N, WiFi:Y, Locker:N, Recep:ltd; Note: TV, books, a/c, near beach

Casa Del Shiva, Calle 2 Nte, Mz 228, Lt 6 y 7, Av 120>125 Nte, Col Ejido; *casadelshiva@live.co.uk*, T:+52.984.859.3557, *facebook.com/Casadelshivahostel/*; $13Bed, Pvt.room:Y, Kitchen:Y, B'fast:Y, WiFi:Y, Locker:Y, Recep:24/7; Note: tents OK, pool, resto, bikes, wh/chair OK, not central, tour desk

Hostel Quinta Playa, 2nd St, bet. 5th Ave>Ocean, Playa del Carmen, QR: T:(984)147.0428, *Info@ 5taplaya.com*, $13Bed, Pvt.room:N, Kitchen:Y, B'fast:$, WiFi:Y, Locker:Y, Recep:24/7; Note: pool, resto, minimart, luggage rm, tour desk, tea/coffee, lack window

Hostel 3B, Av. 10 Esq. Calle 1ra. Sur, QR; T:(984)147.12.07, *info@ hostel3b.com/*; $15Bed, Pvt.room:N, Kitchen:Y, B'fast:N, WiFi:Y, Locker:Y, Recep:24/7; Note: bikes, a/c, luggage rm, tour desk, parking, "cheap and chic"

The Yak, Calle 10 Norte Bis, bet. Av. 10 y Av. 15, Playa del Carmen, QR; *yakhostel@gmail.com*, T:+52.984.148.0925, *facebook.com/HostelYak/info/*; $14Bed, Pvt.room:Y, Kitchen:Y, B'fast:Y, WiFi:Y, Locker:Y, Recep:24/7; Note: café/bar, wh/chair OK, luggage rm, tour desk, parking, laundry

Happy Gecko Hostel, 10th Av, Calles 6>8, Playa del Carmen, QR; *happygeckohotel@hotmail.com*, T:+52.984.148.6556, (see FaceBook page); $13Bed, Pvt.room:Y, Kitchen:Y, B'fast:Y, WiFi:Y, Locker:Y, Recep:24/7; Note: bar, billiards, books, tour desk, luggage room, cash only

3 Mundos Hostel, Calle 6 Norte, Ave 20>Ave 25, Playa del Carmen, QR; *tresmundoshostel.com/*, T:(984)147.0506, *tresmundoshostel@hotmail.com*; $8Bed, Pvt.room:Y, Kitchen:Y, B'fast:Y, WiFi:Y, Locker:Y, Recep:ltd; Note: bikes, luggage rm, tour desk, parking, laundry, tea/coffee, books

Colores Mexicanos Hostel, 15 Ave, bet. 2nd St/Juarez Av., P. del Carmen; *hostelcolores_mexicanos@hotmail.com*, +52.984.873.0065, (see FB page); $12Bed, Pvt.room:Y, Kitchen:Y, B'fast:N, WiFi:Y, Locker:Y, Recep:8a>9p; Note: wheelchair OK, parking, luggage rm, TV, courtyard, nr beach/center

Maria Sabina Hotel/Backpackers, Calle 6Nte #796, col.Centro, P. Carmen; *mariasabinahotel.com/*, T:+52.984.873.0113, *mariasabinahotel@gmail.com*; $10Bed, Pvt.room:Y, Kitchen:N, B'fast:$, WiFi:Y, Locker:Y, Recep:24/7; Note: tour desk, luggage room, a/c, arpt trans $, TV, fax, nr beach/bus

TULUM is a town of over 18,000 near the ruins of the same name, famous for its beachside Caribbean setting. Tulum Pueblo has grown from almost nothing to a service town of restaurants, bars, equipment rentals, and nightlife. The 'hotel zone' is rustic, refreshingly so. It was even more rustic thirty years ago, with vans camped on the beach.

Posada Los Mapaches, opp. Ruinas Tulum, Tulum, Fed Hwy 307, Q.R; *posadalosmapaches.com/*, T:+52.984.871.2700, *posadalosmapaches@gmail.com*; $19Bed, Pvt.room:Y, Kitchen:N, B'fast:Y, WiFi:Y, Locker:Y, Recep:ltd; Note: bikes, books, maps, safe dep, beach, 2N min

Hostel Sheck, Satelite Norte/Sagitario, Tulum, QR; *hostelsheck.com/*, T:+52.984.133.3992; $13Bed, Pvt.room:N, Kitchen:Y, B'fast:Y, WiFi:Y, Locker:Y, Recep:8a>11p; Note: central, bar, luggage rm, tour desk, cash only

Hostal Chalupa, Av. Tulum/Av. Coba, Tulum; *chalupahostal@hotmail.com*, T:+52.984.871.2116, (see Facebook page); $17Bed, Pvt.room:Y, Kitchen:Y, B'fast:Y, WiFi:Y, Locker:Y, Recep:ltd; Note: pool, bar, bikes, books, luggage rm, parking, tour desk, edge of town

Casa Del Sol Mexico, No. 815 Polar Pte, bet. Saturno Y Luna Nte, Tulum, QR: *casadelsolhostels.com/*, T:+52.984.129.6424, *twitter.com/CasaDelSolTulum*; $13Bed, Pvt.room:Y, Kitchen:Y, B'fast:Y, WiFi:Y, Locker:N, Recep:24/7; Note: bikes, books, terrace, luggage rm, parking, tour desk, basic

Weary Traveler Hostel, Tulum 36, Tulum QR: *Reservations@wearytravelerhostel.com/*, T:+52.984.871.2390; $12Bed, Pvt.room:Y, Kitchen:Y, B'fast:Y, WiFi:Y, Locker:N, Recep:ltd; Note: beach shuttle, constant party, central, near bus

Jardin De Frida, Av Tulum (bet. Kukulkan/Chemuyil, opp. Camello JR; *fridastulum.com/*, T:+52.984.871.2816, *fridastulum@gmail.com*; $18Bed, Pvt.room:Y, Kitchen:Y, B'fast:Y, WiFi:Y, Locker:Y, Recep:ltd; Note: resto/bar, bikes, minimart, luggage rm, parking, tour desk, eco-J

El Punto, Av Coba Sur y calle Mercurio, Tulum, QR, T:+52.984.807.9387, *contact@ tulumsolhotel.com/*; $14Bed, Pvt.room:Y, Kitchen:Y, B'fast:N, WiFi:Y, Locker:N, Recep:24/7; Note: luggage rm, parking, laundry, bikes, near beach

62) Sinaloa

MAZATLAN is a city of 440,000 in the state of Sinaloa along the Mexican Pacific coast. It sits right on the edge of the tropics, so the weather is good year-round, with rare possibilities for some cold weather. There is a designated tourist zone. There is a carnival. There is a ferry to La Paz, BC. There are international flights to the US. I haven't been there in about thirty years. Maybe I'll go next week. I'm serious.

Funky Monkey Hostel, 112 Cerro Boludo, Mazatlan, Sin; T:+52.669.166.6365, *funkymonkeyhostel@yahoo.com*, (see Facebook page); $10Bed, Pvt.room:Y, Kitchen:Y, B'fast:N, WiFi:Y, Locker:N, Recep:ltd; Note: free arpt trans, pool, bikes, forex, hot tub, cash only, parking

63) Veracruz

XALAPA is a city of a half million in the state of Veracruz, and the home of *xala* — oops! I mean *jala* — *penos*, those fat fiery peppers that pickle up so nicely. There is a university, and the culture that brings: theaters, museums, street art, and music and dance in the plaza at night. Sounds fun, no?

Hostal De La Niebla, Gutiérrez Zamora 24, Zona Centro, Xalapa, Veracruz; T:+52.228.817.2174, *delaniebla.com/*; $13Bed, Pvt.room:Y, Kitchen:Y, B'fast:Y, WiFi:Y, Locker:Y, Recep:24/7; Note: café, books, maps, luggage rm, tour desk, terrace

64) Yucatan

MERIDA is a city of about a million people and capital of the Yucatan state. It is at the same time the most Mayan and possibly most European of Mexican cities. There is a sizeable historic center, based on the region's previous wealth from henequen production. It is built on top of the pre-existing Mayan city of Tho, with many of the same building blocks in reuse. The Gulf of Mexico is only 22mi/35km away at Progreso. The splendid Mayan ruins of Uxmal are an easy day trip away. *Cenotes* (underground rivers) dot the rural landscape, sometimes concealing ancient treasure. There are many galleries and museums. The cuisine is unique and tasty, but there's still not much for us vegetarians. The most central of Gulf/Carib cities, Merida is almost equidistant to Houston, New Orleans, Miami, Managua… or Mexico City. Flights are cheaper to Cancun, though, especially from Miami. I once flew from Merida to New Orleans for seventy bucks… a while ago. My first foreign excursion was to here, back in 1975.

Nomadas, Calle 62 #433 por 51, Centro, Mérida, Yuc; *nomadastravel.com/*, T:+52.999.924.5223, *nomdashostel1@hotmail.com*; $8Bed, Pvt.room:Y, Kitchen:N, B'fast:Y, WiFi:Y, Locker:Y, Recep:24/7; Note: pool, tour desk, luggage rm, parking

Hostal Palau, Calle 25 A No 498A x 56A y 58 Itzimna, Merida, Yuc; T:+52.999.987.8843, *Info@ hostalpalau.com/*; $11Bed, Pvt.room:Y, Kitchen:Y, B'fast:Y, WiFi:Y, Locker:Y, Recep:24/7; Note: arpt trans, pool, terrace, tour info, 15 min. walk to ctr

Hostel Luna Nueva, Calle 56-a #487 Por 49 Centro, Mérida, Yuc; T:+52.999.923.0482, *lunanuevahostel.com/*; $10Bed, Pvt.room:Y, Kitchen:N, B'fast:Y, WiFi:Y, Locker:Y, Recep:24/7; Note: café, parking, laundry, c.c. OK

Hostel Zocalo, Calle 63 #508, Centro, Mérida, Yuc; *hostalzocalo.com/*, T:+52.999.930.9562; (see FB page); $8Bed, Pvt.room:Y, Kitchen:Y, B'fast:Y, WiFi:Y, Locker:N, Recep:24/7; Note: minimart, forex, tour desk, luggage rm, laundry

La Casa Del Tio Rafa, C. 65 #589 x 72 y 74 Centro, Mérida, Yuc; T:+52.999.924.9446, *lacasadeltiorafa.com/*; $10Bed, Pvt.room:Y, Kitchen:Y, B'fast:Y, WiFi:Y, Locker:Y, Recep:24/7; Note: pool, bikes, wh/chair OK, tour desk, luggage rm, laundry

VALLADOLID is a city of over 45,000 in the interior of Yucatan state. It is one of Mexico's 'Pueblo Magico' cities, recognized for their culture and beauty. It suffered greatly during the 1848 Caste War. Today it is a pleasant city with *cenote* in the center, and convenient base for excursions to the ruins of Chichen Itza or Ek Balam. There are parks, museums, cathedrals, and markets for produce and handicrafts.

Hostel La Candelaria, Calle 35 # 201-F x 42 & 44, Valladolid; *hostelvalladolidyucatan.com/*, T;+52.985.856.2267, *hostel-valladolid@hotmail.com*; $10Bed, Pvt.room:Y, Kitchen:Y, B'fast:Y, WiFi:Y, Locker:Y, Recep:24/7; Note: 30min>Chichen, nr bus stn, bikes, luggage room, parking, terrace

Hostal Del Fraile, Calz. de los Frailes #212-C x 48y50, Col., Valladolid; *hostaldelfraile.com/*, $10Bed, *hdelfraile@gmail.com*; Pvt.room:Y, Kitchen:Y, B'fast:Y, WiFi:Y, Locker:N, Recep:ltd; Note: basic, cafe

65) Zacatecas

ZACATECAS is yet still another of those north-central Mexican colonial gems, of historical beauty and significance, and a UNESCO world heritage designation to prove it. Capital of the state of the same name, it is smaller than the other colonial capitals at only 130,000 — *nice*. It was important for its silver mines, one of which is a tourist attraction within the city limits today. The Bufa hill is the preeminent landmark. Its narrow streets and facades place it on a "Trail of Silver" with Taxco and Guanajuato.

Hostal Villa Colonial, Primero de Mayo #201, Centro Histórico, Zacatecas; *ihostels.com/*, T:+52.492.922.1980, *hostalvillacolonial@gmail.com*; $9Bed, Pvt. room:Y, Kitchen:Y, B'fast:$, WiFi:Y, Locker:Y, Recep:24/7; Note: arpt trans, café/bar, central, luggage rm, tour desk, laundry, hist. bldg

About the Author

American Hardie Karges took his first extended international trip at the age of twenty-one in 1975 and traveled to his first ten countries within two years, all for less than two thousand dollars. Thus began a way of life that has taken him to some one hundred fifty countries (and counting), living and working in a dozen of them, learning several languages and trading in folk art and cottage industry products. He has also published poetry and created videos, before finally deciding to write about what he knows best—travel. His first book, "Hypertravel: 100 Countries in 2 Years," was published in 2012. The full set of "Backpackers & Flashpackers" (Hostel Guides to the World) is projected to include six to eight volumes and be completed in 2014.

If you would like more information, or to make an inquiry or just leave a comment, please visit our blog at *backpackers-flashpackers.net/* or our *BackpackersFlashpackers* page on FaceBook.